Recession-Proof Your Retirement Years

Simple Retirement Planning Strategies
That Work Through Thick or Thin

STEVE VERNON, FSA

Rest-of-Life Communications
Oxnard, California

Recession-Proof Your Retirement Years - Simple Retirement Planning Strategies That Work Through Thick or Thin

Fourth edition February 2014

ISBN-13: 978-0-9853846-2-3

For additional copies, visit www.restoflife.com or send an email to steve.vernon@restoflife.com.

Rest-of-Life Communications
3600 Harbor Blvd., Suite 110-115
Oxnard, CA 93035

www.restoflife.com
steve.vernon@restoflife.com

Hello friends!

Are you worried about having enough money to last throughout your retirement years? Are you concerned about potentially racking up costly bills for medical or long-term care expenses that drain your savings? Are you wondering how you can truly enjoy your so-called "golden years"?

You're not alone. Thousands of people across the country are concerned about just how they're going to be able to make it during their retirement years, especially given the current state of our economy. Many of us got slammed by the stock market crash and economic downturn of 2008-2009. What now? Will a comfortable retirement end up being just a fantasy?

I'm Steve Vernon, and I worked as a consulting actuary for more than 35 years, helping Fortune 500 employers and other large organizations design and manage their retirement programs. Now I help people prepare for their retirement years, or *rest-of-life*, as I like to call it. I advocate simple, realistic strategies to help you manage your money, health and lifestyle that should work through thick or thin.

I don't tell you how to retire to Panama, Mexico or some other exotic location; get rich by investing in gold, real estate, collectibles, options or commodities; retire at 50 to a life of luxury; or use sophisticated estate-planning strategies that are really meant for the more affluent among us.

Instead, I advocate using simple retirement planning strategies that are practical and realistic for most working Americans. No more, no less. I'm offering no gimmicks and no flashy techniques that may sell books but won't work for the average American.

There's no use hiding the fact that we face significant challenges when it comes to our retirement years. But instead of being depressed and paralyzed about these trends, I'd rather move forward as best as we can, using strategies and techniques that are practical and realistic. If this sounds like a good plan with respect to your retirement years, I'll show you how to get on track, using the latest research and solid financial analyses. I'll describe how to increase your odds of living a long, prosperous life and help prepare you for a future that's certain to have more ups and downs.

Take charge of the rest of your life, and you'll put a lot of anxieties to rest! If you're ready, let's get started.

TABLE OF CONTENTS

"If we take a late retirement and an early death, we'll just squeak by."

At least he's planning! This book shows you a better plan.

SECTION I

INTRODUCTION AND PREPARATION

If you're anywhere close to retiring, chances are good your radar picks up on the many stories and advertisements out there about how to retire comfortably. And while there's a lot of good information being published, there are also many ideas that may not work for you or are simply self-serving hype.

Confused or worried about retirement? You're not the only one. Thousands of people nationwide are wondering just how they're going to be able to retire comfortably, especially given the current state of our economy. So how do you decide what to do and what will work best for your particular situation? Let me tell a personal story that offers some ideas and insights.

Late in 2008, I had dinner with my mother who was 87 at the time, and I asked her how she was doing, given the financial meltdown. "I'm doing just fine," she told me, "but I'm worried about what you kids will inherit, since the value of my retirement investments has dropped a lot." I told her that "we kids" don't worry about our inheritance and are much more interested in her well-being. She lived to age 92, and never worried about running out of money.

I delved a little deeper to find out more about why she did so well. What can you learn from this? Plenty! Let's take a look:

- She had a lifetime pension from my father, who worked until age 65 as a professor at USC. That pension and her Social Security income just kept chugging along, in spite of the economic meltdown.
- She supplemented her pension and Social Security benefits with interest and dividend income from her retirement investments. While the value of her stocks had dropped significantly, the amount of her dividend income dropped by a smaller, tolerable amount.
- She paid off the mortgage on her house. The house is small by today's standards, but it met her needs just fine.
- She kept her living expenditures low and had no credit card debt. She drove a seven-year-old car, and kept it for the rest of her life.
- She stayed in good health; she ate sparingly—but consumed lots of fruits and vegetables, and she exercised by walking and gardening. She even grew some of her own food.
- She volunteered once a week in a nonprofit thrift store. She did the same tasks as if she were working for wages, so she could have found a job that would offer a small paycheck if she needed it.
- She kept in touch with friends and relatives, and saw family members at least once a week (all of her kids lived nearby).

The financial meltdown really hadn't changed her life very much. She still had about the same income and expenses, and she continued to do what gave her joy in life. After talking with her, I realized that she and my late father made some smart choices that recession-proofed their lives, managing to successfully navigate through four downturns since my father retired in 1981.

It was that conversation with my mother that really inspired this guidebook. I was relieved to learn that my mom and dad had planned well for their retirement years. But I also knew there were many people out there who hadn't done as well. I wanted to write a book that would offer people in their 50s, 60s and 70s a systematic plan for living a long, prosperous life—and for surviving future downturns (which are inevitable). Having good strategies in place can help dispel the natural fear and anxiety that we all feel about the future. And it helps us focus on what's really important—reaching our full potential during our retirement years, taking care of unfinished business, spending time with friends and family, and passing along our legacy.

Of course, the goal is easy to say, a lot harder to do: You want enough income to cover your living expenses for the rest of your life, no matter how long you live and no matter what happens with the economy. At all costs, you want to prevent being broke at age 85 when you can't push "rewind" on your life or your finances. Many financial planners focus on building wealth; this is a different problem from developing reliable sources of income in your retirement years, which is what I'll show you how to do in this book.

To stack the odds against the risk of outliving your money, I'll share ten smart steps you can take to recession-proof your retirement years. The information in this guidebook will then help you navigate through these steps and achieve the type of retirement you really want. This guidebook will:

- Help you prepare for your retirement/*rest-of-life* by using simple strategies that should work through thick or thin.
- Introduce a systematic, realistic plan for addressing retirement risks and preventing common mistakes.
- Point you in the right direction for additional resources. You'll need to do more than just read this guidebook.
- Help you take action steps while you're still working to plan for a successful retirement.
- Offer realistic strategies regarding money, health and lifestyle, and show how each affects the others.

There's no use hiding the fact that we face significant challenges in our retirement years. Here's one example: The average 401(k) balance for people in their 50s and 60s is about $100,000. This will generate a lifetime income that increases for inflation of roughly $4,000 per year. This won't exactly fund those "golden years" we've all been looking forward to. Add the threat of large medical bills, and you can really get anxious about the future. I've seen the statistics: Somewhere between 30 million and 50 million older Americans are in this predicament. But instead of worrying about these challenges, you can take action. And that's what this guidebook can help you do.

> *"Action is the antidote to despair."*
>
> — **Joan Baez**

In spite of the challenges we face, I believe it's a good time to be aging. There's plenty of scientific and medical research that shows us how to live long, healthy lives. Social research shows what makes us happy and gives us meaning, particularly in our later years. There are many robust, efficient financial products and services, as well as nonprofit organizations that advocate for seniors and provide helpful resources. And all of these resources are at our fingertips because of the internet. None of these resources were available to our parents' generation, so we've got a tremendous head start. It's just up to us to make the best of what we've got.

What Does It Mean to Recession-Proof Your Retirement Years?

There are several things you need to understand in order to make the best plans for your *rest-of-life:*

- You can't prevent a recession, depression or high inflation from happening. That's out of your control.
- You can't even prevent these events from causing some damage to your finances. That's unrealistic.
- You *can* adopt strategies that will help you survive these events, so they don't cause you permanent damage and you can hold on until the economy recovers.
- You'll need to protect against other risks as well.

Over the span of the past 27 years, there have been four major downturns:

- The 1987 stock market crash
- The savings and loan crisis of the early 1990s
- The bursting of the tech bubble that lasted from 2000 to 2002
- The stock market crash and economic downturn of 2008-2009

Those of you with longer memories may also remember the stock market crash of 1974-1975 and the high inflation of the late 1970s.

Economic downturns and calamities happen—they're simply inevitable. And since you'll most likely be retired for 20 years or more, it would be wise to prepare for future crises, since one or more is bound to happen at some point in your retirement years. This guidebook provides a systematic plan to help you survive future economic challenges and minimize the damage, so you can focus on enjoying life.

Top 10 Retirement Mistakes

When it comes to retirement, one of the worst mistakes people make is neglecting to plan ahead. Instead, they just "wing it" with regard to drawing down their retirement savings. They take out what they need for living expenses and hope their money will last. Well, hope is not a good strategy!

Instead, you've got to have a plan. You've got to carefully consider just what your retirement needs will be in order to make sure you don't run out of money. You don't want you or your loved ones to become destitute in your 80s while you still have some good years of life ahead of you. A good plan will help you avoid this fate.

By planning ahead, you may be able to avoid these **Top 10 Retirement Mistakes**:

1. Not creating a realistic assessment of financial resources. Half of all older workers haven't calculated what they need for retirement or budgeted for retirement expenses.
2. Retiring too early with insufficient financial resources. This is a natural consequence of not preparing a financial-needs analysis. And an increasing reliance on 401(k)/account-based plans presents a significant challenge. The average 401(k) account balances of older Americans are far from sufficient to fund an adequate lifetime income.
3. Starting pension benefits too early. Most workers retire before maximizing their retirement income.
4. Starting Social Security benefits too early. Half of all Americans start taking benefits at age 62, the earliest possible age that generates the lowest amount of monthly income.
5. Drawing down 401(k)/retirement savings too rapidly. Withdrawing just 4% to 5% per year is considered a safe withdrawal percentage, but many people withdraw at much higher rates.
6. Uninformed or poor selection of financial advisors and/or products. Choosing unwisely can seriously affect how much money your investments earn.
7. Tapping home equity too early through home equity loans or reverse mortgages. You might need that money later in life if you need long-term care.
8. Continuing an unhealthy lifestyle. Doing so increases your chances of developing expensive, debilitating conditions.
9. Not having strategies in place for medical and long-term care expenses. You don't want these expenses to wipe out your retirement savings.
10. Having living expenditures that are unnecessary, unrealistic or unaffordable, given all the above mistakes. You don't want to run out of money in your later years and then regret buying things that weren't really necessary or important.

And here's one more, thrown in for good measure:

Not having a good idea of what you want to do in your retirement years!

Which brings us to the next set of lists…

Good and Bad Reasons to Retire

GOOD REASONS TO RETIRE	BAD REASONS TO RETIRE
You have a good idea of what you want to do with your time, or you have a plan to find out. You've prepared a strong financial plan, and you have sufficient financial resources.	You're bored with or sick of work. You got laid off. You don't like your boss. Your friends are retiring. Retirement is what you're supposed to do at your age. Your parents retired at your age. You think you have enough money, though you don't really know for sure.

HOMEWORK ITEM: ***Determine your reasons for retiring.*** This is a great topic to discuss with your spouse, partner or close friends and family. Talking through important issues with people who care about you is an excellent way to help you make difficult decisions. Having good reasons to retire and avoiding the bad reasons gets you off to a great start.

Hopes and Dreams vs. Fears and Concerns

Before we go any further, let's do an exercise I like to call "**Hopes and Dreams vs. Fears and Concerns**." I want you to take five minutes and list out all the hopes and dreams you have for the future. What do you want to do with your time? Do you want to travel? Do you have hobbies or interests you want to pursue? How would you like to be remembered? This list is the first step you'll take towards living the life you want. One poignant way to complete this exercise is to write your obituary, and then vow to live up to it.

Then take another five minutes and write out all your fears and concerns about the future. What events or situations might prevent you from realizing your hopes and dreams? What are you most scared will happen to prevent you from living the life you want?

You can use Appendix A at the back of this book to help you create these lists.

HOMEWORK ITEM: ***Share and discuss your lists with your spouse or partner and/or close friends and relatives who care about you.*** Sharing your list gives you the opportunity to get feedback from the people who know you best, people who can help you live the best possible *rest-of-life.*

Now that you've made your list, you can use it as you read and work through this guidebook to evaluate the solutions that are out there. This helps you decide what kind of plans you can make that will help you realize your hopes and dreams and protect against your fears and concerns. Setting your intent to address these issues is a powerful first step.

And with good plans in place, you'll feel more confident that you'll be able to realize your hopes and dreams, and that your fears and concerns won't prevent you from enjoying your life.

HOMEWORK ITEM: ***Visit with older friends and relatives who are doing well in their retirement years.*** Ask them about their secrets to living well in their *rest-of-life.* What steps did they take that they're glad they took? What do they wish they had done differently? You'll learn some good tips, and having good examples to follow helps you make important changes in your own life.

Top 10 Retirement Risks

Understanding the mistakes people make regarding retirement is only the first step toward creating the type of *rest-of-life* you really want. You also need to understand the risks involved with retirement. So let's take a look at this list of **Top 10 Retirement Risks**:

1. Living too long and running out of money
2. Recession/stock market crash that reduces the value of your retirement savings
3. Inflation eroding the value of your fixed pensions and fixed investments
4. Low interest rates that result in reduced income
5. Poor health and resulting high medical bills
6. Potentially ruinous bills for long-term care expenses
7. Reduction in needed wage income during your retirement years
8. Bad advice, fraud or theft
9. Death of your spouse
10. Loneliness, boredom or lack of purpose

Addressing these risks will help you prevent the most common mistakes shown previously. And you can address these risks by implementing the following strategies that will help provide security in your retirement years.

10 Steps to Retirement Security

- Take care of your health.
- Protect against the risk of catastrophic conditions.
- Consider working as long as you can.
- Maximize Social Security income by delaying benefits.
- Be prudent when withdrawing retirement savings.
- Maximize income from traditional pension plans.
- Manage your investment risk and invest for income.
- Adjust living expenses to match your retirement income.
- Develop a robust social portfolio.
- Become a student of retirement and build a professional team.

These steps aren't rocket science; they're mainly common sense. And while all of us should be taking these steps to insure security in our retirement years, many people aren't. The fact is, most people haven't done much planning because they just haven't thought much about their retirement years, or they don't know where to start.

This book removes the mystery surrounding retirement planning, so you can apply your common sense. Planning wisely for your *rest-of-life* simply means making every dollar count and using ***all*** the resources available to you—financial and nonfinancial.

Section II of this guidebook will provide the details you need to implement these 10 steps. But before we go there, let's cover a few more important issues.

Just How Much Life Do You Have Left?

When it comes to your *rest-of-life*, there's really a lot at stake. Studies from the Society of Actuaries estimate the life expectancies for men as shown in Table 1:

Table 1. Life Expectancies for Men

CURRENT AGE	EXPECTED REMAINING YEARS	EXPECTED AGE AT DEATH
50	31	81
55	27	82
60	22	82
65	18	83
70	14	84

Source: RP-2000 mortality table

Here's the same table for women:

Table 2. Life Expectancies for Women

CURRENT AGE	EXPECTED REMAINING YEARS	EXPECTED AGE AT DEATH
50	34	84
55	29	84
60	25	85
65	21	86
70	17	87

Source: RP-2000 mortality table

Doesn't knowing that you may have twenty to thirty years left inspire you to want to make the most of those years? Isn't it worth spending some time now planning to get it right? Here's one way to look at it: Why not spend the same amount of time you'd take planning your next vacation and plan for your *rest-of-life*—a time span much longer than the typical two-week vacation?

The above tables also just show the *average* years remaining for both healthy and unhealthy people, all mixed together. Can you beat the averages? Absolutely! If you make a few lifestyle changes (eat right, get enough exercise, manage stress, stop smoking), you can improve your odds and add another five to seven years to your life expectancy. On the other hand, if you continue unhealthy habits, you can tip the time frames in the other direction and actually *subtract* five to seven years from your expected lifespan!

This knowledge should motivate you to make the necessary lifestyle changes that will enable you to live longer, live healthier and spend less money on medical and long-term care expenses. And a great "side" benefit is that you'll look and feel better now. The downside? You'll need more money to fund a longer retirement, so that's why you need to consider your lifestyle and finances together when planning for the rest of your life.

> **HOMEWORK ITEM:** ***Estimate your life expectancy by taking your lifestyle and family history into account.*** It can be an eye-opener to many people to learn that your financial resources may need to last a much longer time after you stop working than you had initially thought. Two excellent websites that can help you estimate your life expectancy are www.livingto100.com and www.bluezones.com. The good thing about both of these sites is that they give you tips to put into practice that will help improve your results.

Money Is Not Enough!

When planning for your retirement years, you need to build a financial portfolio that will support your intended lifestyle. But that isn't sufficient for a long, prosperous *rest-of-life*. You must think more broadly and include strategies that will improve your health and lifestyle, too.

These three areas—finances, health and lifestyle—overlap and influence each other throughout our lives, and they're especially critical in our retirement years. For instance, if you don't have your health, then you drain your finances trying to get healthy and you most likely aren't very happy. Another overlap? Studies have shown that if you're happy and satisfied with your life, you're less likely to get sick.

Here's another example: Studies have also shown that money can't buy happiness, yet not having enough money to meet your basic needs can make you unhappy. Also, worry and stress over finances can adversely affect your health, making you "sick with worry."

Finding ways to improve each of these three areas—finances, health and lifestyle—significantly increases the odds of having a long, prosperous life. And while it's not guaranteed, following the strategies outlined in this guidebook should put you in the ballpark. From there, you can always make adjustments as you experience life's twists and turns.

But—and here's the important part—if you're not even close to having sufficient resources, you may not be in the position to guide your destiny. Instead, you'll merely get the life that shows up, which may not be the life that you want.

The Magic Formula

At parties and social situations, once people learn that I'm a consulting actuary who writes about retirement, they often ask me for a magic formula or number that will ***guarantee*** a secure retirement. At last, this actuary is the life of the party!

Back to the question, the operative word here is "magic." Do you believe in magic? I didn't think so. There is, however, an effective formula that you can use to manage your resources for the rest of your life:

$$I > E$$

The first part of the formula is your income (the "I" in the equation above). That'll include such financial sources as Social Security, pensions, savings, 401(k) plans and income from work. The second part of the formula is your expenses (the "E" in the equation above).

For the average American, 75% of their household budget goes toward the following five expenses (in this order):

- Housing
- Transportation
- Food
- Health
- Entertainment

In order to make sure you have sufficient resources for retirement, you've got to determine the right balance between income and expenses, one that will make you happy, both before and during retirement. Throughout the guidebook, I'll provide strategies for maximizing your "I" and minimizing your "E." Section III of this guidebook will help you estimate your "I" and your "E" in your retirement years, using the worksheets I've included in Section IV.

Note: You may want to familiarize yourself now with these worksheets, which will help you better understand the "I" and "E" concepts as you encounter them throughout the guidebook. You can also use online software or spreadsheets instead of the paper worksheets in this book, most of which employ the same concepts as the included worksheets.

Top 10 Retirement Decisions

In addition to understanding your "I" and "E," by the time you're done with this guidebook, you'll also have made great progress toward answering the following questions:

1. How much money will you need during your retirement years?
2. How much should you save between now and the start of your retirement?
3. Will you need (or want) to work in your later years?
4. When should you start taking your lifetime retirement incomes from Social Security and, if applicable, from a traditional pension?
5. How can you draw down your retirement savings so you don't outlive your savings?
6. How can you best manage your living expenses to match your income?
7. What type of investments should you make and how should you allocate your assets?
8. What steps will you take to improve your health?
9. How can you manage the risk of high expenses for medical and long-term care services?
10. What will you do with your time?

Determining the answers to these questions will help you more easily answer the biggest question of all: When can—or should—you retire?

Even if you don't have all the information you need to get the answers you're seeking, realize that getting in the ballpark is a good first step—and is often good enough. And it's certainly much better than doing nothing.

Take Inventory

In preparation for working through the rest of this guidebook, you'll want to take inventory of all your financial resources that might produce income or provide protection against risks in your retirement years. Turn to **Worksheet #1: Retirement Resources Inventory** in Section IV to get started. Be sure to include all your 401(k) balances, IRAs and pension benefits you've earned, as well as your spouse's resources. If you work for a nonprofit or government, include balances in 403(b) and 457 savings plans. Also list all the insurance policies you have that can provide protection in your retirement years, such as life insurance, medical insurance, disability insurance and long-term care insurance. Don't include the value of your house, antiques, jewelry, collectibles, etc. unless you plan to sell them and convert them to assets that can generate income. And if this is the case, be sure to reduce any sales proceeds by estimates of applicable taxes and selling costs.

Another important part of your inventory is your "human capital." While it's not financial in nature, it most certainly affects just how comfortable your *rest-of-life* will be.

Your Human Capital Inventory

- How many friends or relatives can you confide in and discuss important life decisions with?
- How many friends or relatives live nearby and would come to your aid in an emergency?
- Would any of these friends or relatives be able to take care of you if you needed long-term care?
- Do you have friends or relatives with whom you can share resources, such as a car, appliances, tools, etc.?
- With how many friends and relatives do you participate in regular activities that give you enjoyment and meaning in life? Are you "diversified," meaning that you have several good friends in addition to your spouse or partner?
- What social institutions are nearby that can help you and provide social contacts? Include such associations as churches, social organizations, clubs and the like.
- What state and local government organizations or nonprofits are available to provide potentially necessary services?

Please don't overlook these important nonfinancial resources; if financial resources are insufficient to provide the resources you need, your "human capital" may need to be put to good use.

Now we're ready to get started with Section II and the **10 Steps to Retirement Security.** Following these steps will put you on a good path to recession-proofing your retirement years.

Checklist of Action Steps for Introduction and Preparation

- ❑ Identify with whom you can discuss important issues for planning the rest of your life. If you're not doing this now, one good way is to form a small study group of like-minded people.
- ❑ List your reasons for retiring and discuss them with people who care about you.
- ❑ List your hopes and dreams vs. fears and concerns.
- ❑ Using a website, such as www.livingto100.com, www.bluezones.com or something similar, estimate your life expectancy and your spouse's, if you're married.
- ❑ Prepare the financial Retirement Resources Inventory, Worksheet #1 in Section IV.
- ❑ Prepare your "Human Capital Resources Inventory," as described above.

HELPFUL RESOURCES

- If you want to read a statistical analysis of the challenges we face in our retirement years, visit my website www.restoflife.com, go to the page labeled "Articles and Newsletters," and look for the article titled *Statistical Analysis: Why Traditional Retirement Is Out of Reach for Most Baby Boomers... And What We Should Do About It.*
- Websites such as www.livingto100.com and www.bluezones.com can help you estimate your life expectancy.
- A report prepared by the Society of Actuaries addresses retirement risks in more detail. It's titled *Managing Post-Retirement Risks: A Guide to Retirement Planning,* and you view a copy at http://www.soa.org/files/pdf/post-retirement-charts.pdf.

SECTION II

10 STEPS TO RETIREMENT SECURITY

Now that you're prepped and ready to go, let's jump right in and start reviewing the steps you'll need to take to create the type of retirement you've been dreaming of. Putting the steps I've outlined here into action can take considerable time and effort, but it's definitely worth it given how long you might live. And don't stress about doing everything at once. One way to work through the guidebook is to spend a few weeks studying each step and taking the action steps that are appropriate for that step. If you make incremental but steady progress, you'll be able to look back after a few months and see considerable progress.

STEP 1 Take Care of Your Health

There are simple steps you can take regarding nutrition, exercise and stress management that can help you live a long, healthy life. In fact, if you do a good job in these three areas, there's a good chance you could live to age 90 or 95, maybe even 100. Taking steps to remain healthy far into your retirement years protects against these risks:

- Running out of money, because staying healthy reduces the amount you'll spend on medical bills
- Potentially ruinous bills for long-term care expenses, including the cost of a nursing home
- Reduction in wage income. Maintaining your health allows you to work as long as possible.

I strongly believe that impending health issues present as big of a threat to our prosperity and well-being as the lack of adequate financial resources I described in the Introduction. I'm haunted by the thought of millions of baby boomers depleting their 401(k) balances and other financial resources to pay for costly medical and long-term care expenses. And what's really frustrating—but potentially inspiring—is that a large number of these baby boomers could avoid this fate simply by taking better care of their health now.

If you need motivation to improve your health, simply take a look at older friends and relatives who are suffering from a chronic illness. Better yet, make a visit to a nursing home or residential care facility for the elderly. Not only are these places expensive, but I bet you'd much rather live out your days at home than in a similar facility.

Do you want to minimize the odds of needing such care in your later years? I certainly do! My hope is that this guidebook will provide the insights you need to help you and your family remain healthy as long as possible.

My father had dementia in his eighties, which made me fearful that I'd experience the same fate in my later years. But by channeling that fear, I was motivated to take steps to reduce the odds of developing dementia. If you're feeling fearful about experiencing poor health in your later years, I encourage you to use that fear to motivate you to improve your health.

On the positive side, seek out older friends and relatives who are in good health, and ask about their health habits. They can give you great ideas, and their examples will inspire you to improve your health. Better yet, they can give you a picture of how good life can be.

Need more reasons to take care of your health in order to protect your finances? A study done in 2013 by Fidelity Investments estimates that a couple retiring at age 65 will need an average of $220,000 to pay for future medical expenses. $220,000! Of that amount, only $66,000 will be spent on Medicare premiums. The remainder ($154,000) will be spent when you get sick—on Medicare deductibles, copayments and expenses not covered by Medicare. And that amount doesn't even include dental, vision or long-term care expenses, which could make matters worse. Remember also that these numbers are just averages—some people can spend a lot more, while others can spend a lot less. Now that's powerful motivation to keep healthy!

Fortunately, there's good news on the horizon, too. Here's just a sampling of the reams of scientific and medical research that offers smart strategies for leading a long, healthy life.

- The journal *Health Affairs* reports that the most expensive conditions to treat in our later years, in order, are:
    - Heart disease
    - Cancer
    - Trauma
    - Mental disorders
    - Pulmonary conditions
    - Diabetes
    - Hypertension

Fortunately, most of these diseases can be delayed, mitigated or even prevented by a healthy lifestyle.

- The *Journal of the American Medical Association* reports that annual health care costs are 49% lower for individuals who are non-smokers, not obese and who participate in physical activity three days per week.
- The *Journal of the American Medical Association* also reports that chronic illness accounts for 75% of the nation's annual health care costs. The good news? Many of the conditions driving these costs are preventable.
- Here's another report from the *Journal of the American Medical Association*: Ninety percent of all heart disease patients have one or more of following risk factors:
    - Smoking
    - Diabetes
    - High cholesterol
    - High blood pressure

Note that all the above risk factors are directly affected by lifestyle choices regarding diet, exercise and stress.

- The *American Institute for Cancer Research* tells us that 30 to 40% of all cancers are directly linked to dietary and lifestyle choices.
- The *World Cancer Research Fund* tells us that eating at least five servings a day of vegetables and fruits is associated with an approximately 50% reduced risk for cancer compared to the risk associated with eating only one or two servings.
- Dr. Roy Walford, in his book *Beyond the 120 Year Diet,* says "It [osteoporosis] kills 300,000 citizens annually and costs the nation $3.8 billion a year in medical bills. …osteoporosis is almost unknown in societies in which continued high levels of physical activity are customary."
- The *New England Journal of Medicine* reports that patients who were classified as being socially isolated and having a high degree of life stress had more than four times the risk of death from heart disease and from all other causes when compared with people who had low levels of both stress and isolation.

These facts are just a small sampling of a substantial amount of scientific and medical research that shows us how to reduce the odds of contracting the major killer diseases of old age and increase the odds of living a long, healthy life. If you want to learn more about this research, see the list of resources at the end of this step.

It's sobering to realize that our nation as a whole could cut our medical costs in half if we all adopted healthy living habits. That would go a long way towards solving our health-care crisis!

So what can you do to improve your health? Start with these two lists of five items:

Do these:

1. *Adopt a healthy diet*. Make it low fat and include lots of vegetables, fruits and whole grains. Make it "plant based" vs. "meat based." With a meat-based diet, the main ingredient of each meal is a big hunk of meat, and this diet, according to several studies, is killing millions of people. A plant-based diet, on the other hand, includes many more fruits and vegetables than meat. You could even become vegetarian or vegan, although that's not necessary to significantly improve your diet. Another aspect of a healthy diet is to eat the right amounts of food; too many Americans are simply eating more food than is necessary to maintain a healthy weight.
2. *Exercise*. At a minimum, get out there three to four times per week for 30 to 45 minutes per exercise session. Be sure to include the four types of exercise recommended for seniors by the National Institute of Health (NIH): cardiovascular activity, strength, flexibility and balance.
3. *Manage your stress*. You can't avoid stressful events or situations completely, but you *can* take steps to reduce their negative impact on your health. Helpful steps include: (a) exercise, (b) being aware of how your body reacts to stress and learning

techniques to relax, and (c) being aware of events that cause you stress, and reducing or avoiding them and/or modifying your attitude towards these events.

4. *Don't smoke.* This will be difficult if you're already a smoker, but you've got to somehow find the motivation and help you need to take this essential step. Your health depends on it.
5. *Don't abuse alcohol or other substances.* These bad habits are significantly detrimental to your health. As with smoking, please find whatever reason works for you to stop.

Count these:

1. *Body mass index (BMI), which shows healthy ranges of weight for your height.* A BMI between 18 and 25 is considered healthy. To determine yours, go to either www.weightwatchers.com or www.caloriecontrol.org.
2. *Blood pressure.* A blood pressure reading of below 120/80 is considered healthy.
3. *Cholesterol levels.* Desirable cholesterol counts should be below 200 mg/dL (overall) with an LDL of below 130 mg/dL.
4. *Daily servings of fruits and vegetables.* Make sure you get five or more servings of these each day.
5. *Number of days per week you exercise for 30-plus minutes.* You should be out there a minimum of three days per week. More would be even better.

> *"If exercise came in pill form, it'd be the most widely prescribed drug in the world."*
>
> — **Joe Piscatella,** President of the Institute for Fitness and Health, and author of *Take a Load Off Your Heart*

Here's another great suggestion. Take a Health Risk Assessment, or HRA. It's an online questionnaire about your lifestyle and family history that only takes a few minutes. It offers lifestyle suggestions that will improve your health and longevity. You may have these available through your health care provider; if not, here are three great websites that offer free HRAs:

- www.livingto100.com
- www.bluezones.com
- www.realage.com

Many people know what they need to do to improve their health—they just don't seem to get around to it. So it's important to find the emotional support you need to make necessary changes to your nutrition and exercise. One of the best ways is to enlist your spouse or close friends in your efforts. For example, invite them for a regular walk or to sample healthy food.

You can make nutritious eating fun—it doesn't need to feel like deprivation. Making these lifestyle changes is a great step toward improving your future. Plus, you'll look and feel better *now*.

CHECKLIST OF ACTION STEPS FOR STEP 1: TAKE CARE OF YOUR HEALTH

- ❑ Determine how you can improve your diet, exercise routines and stress management. Don't feel pressured to make all the changes at once; incremental improvement can be good enough.
- ❑ Determine your BMI, and have your blood pressure and cholesterol measured.
- ❑ Take a Health Risk Assessment, and implement some of the suggested action steps.

HELPFUL RESOURCES

Books

- *Healthy at 100*, by John Robbins
- *Take a Load Off Your Heart* and *The Road to a Healthy Heart Leads Through the Kitchen,* by Joe Piscatella
- *Discover Wellness: How Staying Healthy Can Make You Rich*, by Dr. Bob Hoffman
- *The Mature Mind: The Positive Power of the Aging Brain,* by Dr. Gene Cohen
- *The Myth of Alzheimer's*, by Dr. Peter Whitehouse
- *Ten Years Younger*, by Dr. Stephen Masley
- *What Healthy People Know: And the 7 Things They Do to Stay Healthy and Live Long,* by Dr. Bob Gleeson
- *The Great Age Guide to Online Health & Wellness,* by Sandy Berger
- *Grain Brain: The Surprising Truth About Wheat, Carbs, and Sugar-Your Brain's Silent Killers,* by David Perlmutter and Kristen Loberg

Websites

- www.realage.com
- www.livingto100.com
- www.bluezones.com
- www.medlineplus.com
- www.webmd.com
- www.nihseniorhealth.com
- www.health.msn.com
- www.caloriecontrol.org
- www.americanheart.org
- www.prevention.com

STEP 2 Protect Against the Risk of Catastrophic Conditions

If you're already in good health, you're one step ahead when it comes to leading a healthy *rest-of-life*. But even if you're in good health now, you'll still need to protect against the risk of catastrophic conditions that could affect you as you age. Doing so helps protect you against these risks:

- Running out of money, because having health insurance reduces the amount you'll spend on medical bills
- Running up potentially ruinous bills for long-term care expenses, including the cost of a nursing home

So where do you start? The first step is to get adequate medical insurance. If you're working, you may be able to obtain it through your employer, who might also contribute to the cost of coverage. This could be a good reason to keep working as long as you can. If you're seeking to get it on your own, you may run into roadblocks due to high premiums before age 65. In the "Medical Insurance Options Before Age 65" section below, I've listed a few options you have for obtaining insurance. Unfortunately, for many people who can't afford medical insurance on their own before age 65, their only option may be to continue working in order to secure medical insurance coverage.

Once you're 65, you're eligible for Medicare, which pays for roughly one-half to two-thirds of your medical bills. And while you'll most likely want supplemental insurance to have maximum coverage, your premiums for supplemental insurance will reduce significantly after age 65.

The Basic Facts About Medicare

Although not everyone can afford medical coverage before the age of 65, after that, it's a different story. That's when Medicare kicks in, a lifesaver for many people who could not otherwise afford medical coverage. So let's talk about Medicare for a minute.

There are three parts to Medicare: Part A, Part B and Part D. Medicare Part A covers expenses incurred at hospitals and related facilities. Everyone covered under Social Security is eligible for Part A at age 65. If you or your spouse paid FICA (Federal Insurance Contributions Act) taxes for at least 40 calendar quarters (10 years), you won't have to pay a premium for this coverage. These are payroll taxes collected for Social Security—FICA is simply the tax provision of the Social Security Act. If you and your spouse didn't pay FICA taxes for at least 40 calendar quarters, you can purchase Medicare Part A coverage by paying a monthly premium, as follows:

- If you paid FICA taxes for 30-39 calendar quarters, the monthly premium in 2014 is $234.
- If you paid FICA taxes for fewer than 30 calendar quarters, the monthly premium in 2014 is $426.

Homework Item: ***Determine if you or your spouse paid FICA taxes for at least 40 calendar quarters.*** You can do this by looking at your online summary that Social Security maintains for you. If you haven't paid FICA taxes for at least 40 quarters, determine how much longer you'd need to continue working (and paying FICA taxes) to meet this requirement.

Medicare Part B is medical insurance, covering expenses for physicians and related services. Technically this coverage is optional, since any eligible person who wants it must pay a monthly premium to obtain it. For all practical purposes, however, this coverage is required, particularly if you want to buy insurance to supplement Medicare (which is usually a good idea). For 2014, the standard monthly premium is $104.90, a good deal for most people. Note: A higher monthly premium may apply to certain high-income retirees.

The other part to Medicare is the prescription drug plan, or Part D. Coverage is optional and requires a monthly premium depending on the plan you choose. Premiums commonly range from $30 to $40 per month. The standard design for Part D benefits only provides meaningful benefits for catastrophic drug claims, as shown by the following table.

Table 3. Annual Costs in 2014 Under Standard Design for Part D Prescription Drugs Under Medicare

FOR TOTAL DRUG COSTS BETWEEN...	YOU PAY...	UP TO ...	TOTAL POTENTIAL OUT-OF-POCKET COSTS (NOT INCLUDING PREMIUMS)
$0 and $310	100%	$310	$0 to $310
$310 - $2,850	25%	$635	$310 to $945
$2,850 - $6,455	100%	$3,605	$945 to $4,550
Over $6,455	5%	No limit	$4,550 plus 5% over $6,455

Here's a potential rude awakening: Suppose you're on lifetime maintenance drugs for high blood pressure, high cholesterol, diabetes or other chronic conditions. While you're an active employee, it's likely your medical insurance plan at work will cover most of the cost of these drugs. Under standard Medicare Part D benefits, however, your *annual* out-of-pocket costs could easily be $1,000, $2,000 or more, not including the monthly premiums which can add another $300 to $500 per year.

You might be able to buy prescription drug coverage that's more generous than the standard design, but that will cost you a lot more in premiums. All this money might be better spent elsewhere—but only if it's safe for your health.

Now for the Good News

Many of the conditions that require lifetime maintenance drugs are the result of poor lifestyle choices and habits, like eating the wrong foods and too much of them, smoking or not exercising. Don't get me wrong: I know that in many situations, lifetime maintenance prescription drugs are lifesavers and may be the only solution to a serious health problem. However, I also know many people whose doctor has taken them off these drugs because their test results show they're now in a safe range as a result of lifestyle improvements they've made.

There are two things you can do immediately to start saving money on your medical expenses. First, ask your doctor about generic drugs or alternative prescriptions that might be cheaper and yet still work for you. Second, shop around, because prices vary significantly for the same drugs at different pharmacies (see www.destinationrx.com and www.crbestbuydrugs.org for shopping tips and help).

A longer-range solution is to ask your doctor about participating in a medically supervised lifestyle program to safely wean you off lifetime maintenance drugs; addressing such issues as high blood pressure, high cholesterol, smoking or obesity with a doctor's help can improve your health and help you save money.

But don’t stop there. Don't forget about the things you can do on your own. In Step 1 in this book, I offered many tips that can help you improve your health. Take another look at those suggestions and see which of them you can start implementing now to get on the road to better health.

There are two other parts to Medicare you should know about. Medicare Advantage (MA) provides coverage for both Parts A and B through an HMO or PPO-type provider. There are different plans available in different parts of the country, and some plans offer additional benefits and lower out-of-pocket costs. There are also Medigap plans, which offer supplemental insurance through a third-party provider. The point of Medigap is to fill in gaps that exist from having Medicare coverage. For more information on everything Medicare, go to www.medicare.gov.

Medical Insurance Options Before Age 65

When it comes to obtaining medical insurance before Medicare eligibility at age 65, there's both good news and bad. The good news is, under the Affordable Care Act, you may be able to find the coverage you need without worrying about exclusions for pre-existing conditions. The bad news is, it may cost you a lot.

As an alternative to individually purchased insurance, you may want to exhaust your COBRA coverage first. COBRA coverage allows you to continue your coverage under your employer’s medical plan by paying a higher premium for as many as 18 months after you retire from your job.

The COBRA monthly premium—or the amount you’d be charged to continue coverage—is 102% of the actual cost for active employees; monthly premiums can range from $300 to $500 or more for one person—more for a family. While that may sound high, it's typical: Most employers subsidize health-care coverage for active employees. To continue COBRA coverage, you’ll be paying the full freight of the insurance with no subsidy from your employer.

Some states may have more generous insurance continuation laws than COBRA. Be sure to investigate your options by checking with your state’s insurance department.

As a last resort, some people may be eligible to purchase individual medical coverage or participate in state-sponsored high-risk pools under the Health Insurance Portability and Accountability Act (HIPAA). These plans may be changing under the Affordable Care Act; if this is of interest to you, check for the latest developments in your state.

Shopping for Coverage

As you think about getting the coverage you need for your retirement years, here are some other things to consider:

- You can decrease premiums substantially through:
  - High annual deductible ($2,500, $3,000 or $5,000)
  - High co-insurance (30% to 40%)
  - High out-of-pocket limit ($5,000, $7,500 or more)
- Are you going to sign up for a PPO or an HMO?
- Are your doctors in the network?

One strategy to consider is to be serious about doing all you can to take care of your health, and then just purchase catastrophic coverage with a high deductible and a high out-of-pocket limit. This has the lowest premiums and can save you a substantial amount of money, and you'll still be covered for the potential catastrophic conditions.

If you're ready to start your research into coverage in your retirement years, check out these resources:

- Online quote services, such as www.ehealthinsurance.com and www.insure.com.
- A local insurance agent or broker. Look for someone with experience in selling individual health policies and who shops for the best deal among several insurance companies. And be sure to investigate insurance companies in the state where you plan to live. An independent agent with knowledge of the local market can be a big help.
- State-run or federal health insurance exchanges under the Affordable Care Act that operate in your state.

Also be sure to ask friends and relatives about their experiences with different health plans. And contact accreditation agencies and consumer groups to get feedback on any companies you're considering. Finally, call your state insurance department to check on complaint statistics for any company you're considering using.

When you have your choices narrowed to just a few, compare premiums, deductibles or co-pays, out-of-pocket limits and coinsurance percentages. Read through all the fine print carefully. If you plan to move in the future, make sure you can transfer the policy.

When you're budgeting for health-care expenses, don't forget to factor in the following costs:

- Premiums
  - For you and your spouse
  - For Medicare after age 65 including Parts B and D
- Out-of-pocket
  - Deductibles and co-pays
  - Expenses not covered by insurance

One smart tip is to determine your maximum out-of-pocket expenses under your medical insurance plan and then have this in an emergency savings account.

One last note about health care: If you or a loved one ends up needing medical care, it's important to learn as much as you can about the specific condition. There can be effective alternative or complementary treatments that improve the outcome, and you can learn about them from reliable sources on the internet. Then, have an informed discussion with your physician, which can increase the odds of recovery and potentially reduce the costs of treatment. I have several friends and relatives who have avoided expensive and intrusive surgery or lifetime prescription drugs by informing themselves of alternative treatments, and then discussing the pros and cons with their doctor.

> *"In the United States, over half of people aged 85 and older have dementia or Alzheimer's disease. This kind of impairment causes a lot of loss and grief to individuals and their families. But in many cultures, Alzheimer's and other forms of dementia are rare, even for people in their 90s, and even for people close to 100. And what is the difference? There are differences in diet, exercise, and the web of community support, and significant differences in the respect and esteem that people in their later years receive."*
>
> — **John Robbins,** author of *Healthy at 100*

Should You Buy Long-Term Care Insurance?

I'm asked this question often at my workshops and presentations, and it's a critical one to think about as you near retirement. I'm sorry to say, though, there's no simple answer.

Addressing the threat of potentially ruinous long-term care expenses could be one of the most difficult challenges facing you in your retirement years. And while long-term care insurance may not be the answer for everybody, I strongly advocate that everybody *does* need to have a strategy to address the threat of long-term care expenses.

What Is Long-Term Care?

You'll need to consider getting long-term care when you can't complete ordinary, daily living activities such as bathing, using the bathroom, preparing your own meals or following medical directives, including taking prescription drugs.

There's a wide range of alternatives and costs for long-term care services:

- **Low costs:** Your spouse, family or friends pitch in and take care of you (*if* they're willing and able). The type of assistance you'd need and the time involved varies widely, from minutes to hours each day.
- **Low to medium costs:** Home health care, where care providers come periodically to your home to help you as you need.
- **Medium costs:** Adult day care or a live-in caregiver. Adult day care can work well for situations where 24/7 care isn't needed or if household members have full-time jobs and aren't able to be there when necessary. A live-in caregiver can work if you have a spare bedroom or two and don't mind someone living with you; you can offer room and board and a modest salary. Note that this last approach requires special attention to taxes on the caregiver's salary.
- **High costs:** Nursing homes, assisted living facilities or residential care facilities for the elderly. Costs for these can range from $3,000 to $8,000 per month or more. At this rate, it won't take long to wipe out your retirement savings. If you have the funds or long-term care insurance, however, this is one option to consider.

To make sure we're all on the same page, let's get the terms straight with these high-cost alternatives. Nursing homes are institutions with sick "patients" who need focused medical attention. Assisted living facilities have "residents" who need help with daily living activities. Some institutions combine features of both; you start in the assisted living wing, then if your health declines, you move to a wing that's more like a nursing home. Residential care facilities for the elderly (RCFEs) are licensed houses in regular neighborhoods that are home to a handful of senior citizens, typically up to six, with a staff that takes care of them. RCFEs generally have lower costs than institutional nursing homes and assisted living facilities, with the potential for a living situation that feels more like a home. Like anything else, there are good and bad instances of each type of facility, and you need to do your shopping carefully.

Why Would You Need Long-Term Care?

There are two primary reasons you may need long-term care in your future. The first is health related: If you're in poor health and can't take care of yourself, you're going to have to find some help. The conditions that typically require long-term care and put people into high-cost facilities include Alzheimer's disease, dementia, advanced osteoporosis or simple frailty of old age. These conditions manifest themselves over time; usually there's a long period of onset accompanied by agonizing debate among family members regarding the need for long-term care. The good news is, these conditions can be delayed, mitigated or even prevented altogether with a healthy lifestyle—yet another reason to make your health a high priority.

The other contributing factor is the availability (or lack thereof) of family or friends who can help take care of you. In our grandparents' day, families weren't dispersed across the country, and family members often took care of their frail relatives. These days, having family nearby to help out puts you in the minority. Unfortunately, formal long-term care may be the only solution for people whose health has deteriorated and with no family nearby.

What Can You Do About Long-Term Care Expenses?

The fact is, medical insurance policies and Medicare don't pay for most long-term care expenses. And given our current lifestyles regarding health and the geographic separation of family members, millions of older Americans are vulnerable to the threat of high long-term care expenses. As a consequence, everyone should have a strategy in place to address these costs; that strategy may or may not include some form of long-term care insurance.

Some people think that Medicaid will bail them out if they need long-term care. Think again! Medicaid is a federal program that subsidizes costs for nursing homes and is administered by the states. This subsidy is provided for elderly people who are very sick and who have little or no financial resources. I consider Medicaid facilities to be last resorts, for a number of reasons. First, you need to exhaust your financial resources, leaving you in a precarious financial situation. Second, you need to show significant medical need, and not everybody can meet the requirements. Third, not all facilities accept Medicaid, and the ones that do are often not the most desirable places to live out your last years. Finally, if you do decide to go with a Medicaid facility, you might not get your choice of location, potentially resulting in separation from friends and family.

OK, that's the bad news. But there's good news, too: Long-term care insurance can help provide protection and peace of mind.

If you're considering purchasing long-term care insurance—and I recommend that you give it some serious thought—there are a few things you need to know. Not all policies cover all conditions or types of facilities, so you'll need to pay attention to the fine print to make sure you're getting what you want before you sign on the dotted line. Also, premiums for individually purchased plans are expensive: Annual premiums can range from $1,000 to $4,000 or more if you start in your fifties, depending on the policy's features. As a result, most Americans don't buy this insurance. Or, unfortunately, some people do buy this insurance while they're still working—when they can afford the premiums—but let them lapse when they retire and can no longer afford them.

I would encourage everybody to shop for long-term care insurance as part of your process to develop a strategy for long-term care expenses. See how much the premiums would be, and factor them into your retirement budget. This will help you decide whether you should purchase this insurance or rely on alternative strategies. An internet search will yield good background information on long-term care insurance and alternatives. One good guide comes from the National Association of Insurance Commissioners—see the Resources Section at the end of this step for contact information.

Tips for Buying Long-Term Care Insurance

Should you decide to buy long-term care insurance, here are some tips to read before you do:

- Make sure the insurance company you choose has a lot of experience with long-term care policies. You should look for a company with at least 10 and preferably 20 years of history with this type of insurance.
- Check the insurance company's rating by visiting www.moodys.com and www.standardandpoors.com. I prefer companies with one of the four highest ratings.
- Check to see how many rate increases the insurance company has imposed on existing policy-holders for the past five or 10 years. Several recent rate increases can be a warning flag.
- Look carefully at the fine print to determine when benefits are payable or if there are limitations for pre-existing conditions. I've had family members who were initially denied benefits because they only met five out of six necessary conditions, even though it was clear they were unable to take care of themselves in the way you and I would think necessary.
- Make sure the policy covers a range of care, from home health care to adult day care or nursing homes. Older policies often only covered nursing homes without paying for less expensive and more desirable alternatives.
- Be sure to read the policy carefully before making a commitment, because premiums and related benefits can vary substantially based on the following policy features:
    - The amount of daily benefit payable
    - Whether the daily benefit amount is fixed in dollar terms or if inflation protection is provided
    - The length of the time before benefits are payable but after you've entered the facility or are incurring long-term care expenses (known as the waiting period, the elimination period or the deductible period).
    - How long benefits are payable. Common periods can be for just two years, four years or for your remaining life.

And if you do purchase a policy, don't think that you're home free. The above policy features can substantially limit the benefits that are payable, and you still might need to spend significant, out-of-pocket amounts for long-term care.

Another option is to only buy partial protection with insurance. You can purchase a policy that partially insures against the risk of long-term care by varying the amount of the daily benefit, waiting period, benefit period and inflation protection, and then pay for the rest of your expenses out of pocket.

One final thought: Large employers will often offer group long-term care insurance to their employees. These policies can offer better terms and lower premiums compared to individually purchased policies. If your employer offers this option, check it out.

A Common Scenario for Married Couples

The following situation happens all too frequently with married couples. The husband is the first to need long-term care, since husbands are often older than their wives. In this case, the wife typically becomes the primary caregiver. Eventually the husband passes away, leaving his wife exhausted—both physically and financially. And there's the distinct possibility that nobody is left to care for her, should she need long-term care.

For the reasons cited above, roughly seven out of 10 residents of nursing homes or residential care facilities are women. If you're married and can't afford long-term care premiums for both you and your spouse, a compromise strategy would be to buy insurance just for the wife. However, you need to understand and accept the potential burden this can place on the wife and have strategies in place in case the husband needs long-term care. Also, there's the risk that the wife passes away first, leaving the husband vulnerable. Remember to consider all your options carefully before making your final decision.

Alternatives to Long-Term Care Insurance

If you decide not to buy long-term care insurance, then recognize that at some time in your life, you may need to pay for long-term care expenses with your own money. If you have substantial assets, this may not be a concern to you. However, most people aren't this fortunate, so you should consider one or both of the following strategies:

- Set up a separate savings account that's dedicated to long-term care expenses and won't be tapped to pay for ordinary living expenses. Put into this account the amounts you would have paid for long-term care insurance premiums; over many years, it will add up and you'll have a significant amount set aside when needed.
- If you have substantial home equity, hold your home equity in reserve until you need it for long-term care expenses. At that time, you can tap your equity through a home equity loan, reverse mortgage or simply by selling the home and realizing the profit. Avoid the temptation to take out a reverse mortgage or home equity loan to pay for ordinary living expenses or luxuries during your retirement years, however. And make sure you have a realistic estimate of your home equity, recognizing the potential decline in home values since 2008. Because long-term care expenses can vary widely, you'll need a minimum of $100,000 and preferably $200,000 or more in home equity to rely on this strategy, and that's just for one person. A married couple will most likely need more.

While everybody should get very serious about taking care of their health, this should be even more of a priority for people who don't buy long-term care insurance. You have control of so many things that affect your health, so get started now on the road to better health in order to help eliminate or reduce the need for long-term care later. Healthy steps you take today can eventually save you tens or even hundreds of thousands of dollars down the road!

Let me repeat myself because this is so important: *Everyone should have a strategy in place to address the potential threat of ruinous long-term care expenses.* It's easy to ignore this potential risk when you're in your fifties, sixties or seventies, since the threat seems so far in the future. Resist this temptation! Not only can long-term care be very expensive, but it can be an emotional and exhausting burden on your spouse and children.

CHECKLIST OF ACTION STEPS FOR STEP 2: PROTECT AGAINST THE RISK OF CATASTROPHIC CONDITIONS

- ❑ Determine if you have enough calendar quarters of paying FICA taxes to be eligible for Medicare Part A coverage.
- ❑ If you need medical insurance coverage before age 65, determine how you will get such coverage. Investigate such options as COBRA coverage, individually purchased coverage on an exchange, or coverage through an employer-sponsored plan.
- ❑ Investigate your medical insurance options for coverage supplementary to Medicare after age 65.
- ❑ Develop a budget for premiums and out-of-pocket medical expenses.
- ❑ Develop a strategy for covering long-term care expenses. If this includes long-term care insurance, start shopping for policies now.

HELPFUL RESOURCES

Websites

- www.ehealthinsurance.com and www.insure.com, good places to shop for insurance
- National Association of Insurance Commissioners (www.naic.org) for information on all types of insurance
- National Committee on Quality Assurance (NCQA), which issues "report cards" on accredited plans (www.ncqa.org)
- Joint Commission on Accreditation of Healthcare Organizations (www.jcaho.org), for information on the quality of health care
- American Association of Health Plans offers consumer information on choosing a health plan (www.ahip.org).
- www.healthinsuranceinfo.net offers state-by-state guides on health insurance.
- www.dol.gov/ebsa/faqs offers information on COBRA and HIPAA coverage.
- www.aaltci.org, website of the American Association of Long-Term Care Insurance.
- www.iii.org, the website for the Insurance Information Institute, offers more information on long-term care insurance.

Books

- *A Shoppers Guide to Long-Term Care Insurance*, by the National Association of Insurance Commissioners (www.naic.org)
- *The Insurance Maze*, by Kimberly Lankford provides tips for shopping for all types of insurance, including medical, life, and long-term care insurance.

STEP 3 Consider Working as Long as You Can

There are many reasons for working as long as you can, into your 70s if possible. Here are just a few of the risks you'll protect yourself against if you choose to work into your later years:

- Running out of money. Working longer reduces the pressure on your financial assets and allows you to delay starting Social Security and pension income, which increases the lifetime income from these sources.
- Not having affordable health insurance. Working longer provides a potential for employer-provided health insurance.
- No meaning or purpose in life. Working can provide both, thus protecting you against boredom and loneliness.

What most people really want is to be happy in their later years, and that doesn't necessarily translate into retirement. So can you work a little in your later years and still be happy? And how much money do you really need to be happy?

Continuing to work in your later years doesn't have to be a burden. There are many ways you can make it an enjoyable experience. What about reducing your hours through part-time, project or seasonal work? Or maybe you can hold on to the same job but reduce your hours or responsibilities? What about doing more of what you're good at and like, and less of what you aren't good at or aren't fond of? Maybe you could investigate starting a related career in the same field? Or in a new career field? Or maybe you could start your own business (just don't jeopardize your retirement savings to do this).

Throughout the years, I've seen a number of inspiring examples of older people making work interesting: active people working in sporting goods stores, hobbyists working at hardware stores, photographers working at camera stores, avid readers working at bookstores, moms and grandmoms getting babysitting jobs, former teachers working as tutors, fishers or hunters working as travel guides. With all that's out there, what do you think might work for you?

Working keeps you engaged with life. Need evidence that continuing to work can be a benefit to you? According to a study by the Society of Actuaries, men who were working between the ages of 50 and 70 had roughly half the death rates of men in that age range who weren't working (excluding those on disability). And people aged 50 to 70 with incomes over the poverty level had significantly lower death rates than people with incomes under the poverty level. Maybe working a little in your later years to make ends meet isn't such a bad idea!

Bureau of Labor statistics also offer some interesting insights into the world of work. More than 60 years ago, almost half of all men age 65 and over were in the workforce. That percentage steadily declined to about 15% in the 1990s. Since then, that number's been steadily increasing and is now at just a little more than 20%. Note that these statistics are for *all* men age 65 and older, including men in their 70s, 80s, 90s and beyond. The percentage of men working in their late 60s is much higher than the statistics shown for the entire group. You can make the point that 65 year-olds today are much better able to work than 65 year-olds were 60 years ago. So what was good for our grandfathers might be good for us!

> *"One important reason to work in your retirement years is that it allows you to plug into an automatic social network, which becomes increasingly important in your later years."*
>
> — **John Nelson,** co-author of *What Color is Your Parachute - For Retirement?*

An Alternative to Consider

With traditional retirement, you work full time until your retirement date, and then you retire completely. A more feasible and healthy alternative to consider might be to phase down *earlier* in life, but to keep working *longer* in life. You might want to consider two phases to your retirement years:

Phase 1 would entail a reduction of your working hours and your resulting wage income. This would give you more time to do what you've always wanted to do but couldn't while you were working full time. Your financial resources would supplement your reduced wages only to the extent necessary. This holds your financial resources in reserve until you really need them. You'd focus on doing work that you enjoy and are good at, and reduce or eliminate work that you don't enjoy or aren't good at. This first phase might last until your 70s or later—as long as you can work and enjoy it.

Phase 2 would be a transition to a complete withdrawal from work and an exclusive reliance on your financial resources. This phase might start in your mid-70s or later, or at a point when you're no longer able to work.

Given the financial resources that are available to most baby boomers today, I believe this lifestyle is more practical and realistic than retiring completely in your 50s or 60s. I also believe it can be more fulfilling and healthy than an early, full-time retirement. Compared to traditional retirement, it might be a better way to realize your hopes and dreams—and prevent your fears and concerns from becoming a reality.

Here's one challenge I hear about quite frequently: An older worker likes his or her current job but doesn't want to ask about part-time work for the fear of losing respect among co-workers or for appearing to have low commitment to the job. I acknowledge this can be a real possibility. But let's say you found the courage to inquire and your employer agreed to a reduction in hours. In this case, you'd want to demonstrate with your subsequent actions on the job that you're just as committed and productive as when you worked full time; over time, your co-workers and supervisor would see that you're as committed as when you worked full time.

Another possible strategy to address this challenge is "stealth" reduced hours. You'd keep your full-time status but simply take more time off than you're entitled under your vacation policy. You'd then be taking unpaid leave, which can result in the same income as formal part-time work. Of course, you'd need the buy-in of your supervisor, but this might be a win-win idea if your employer has predictable slow seasons during which you could reduce your hours. If you like your current job but want to reduce your hours, it never hurts to ask about your options!

Whatever you do, don't make the mistake of retiring while you can still work and then depleting your financial resources at an age when returning to work isn't possible. In this weaker economy, I realize that you might get laid off and decide to declare yourself "retired." While I understand why you might want to do this, it's not a good idea if your financial resources are inadequate. If this happens, redouble your efforts to find meaningful work; easier said than done, I know, but still possible. By bouncing back from a layoff, there are benefits to your physical and emotional health in addition to the obvious financial advantages.

There's a basic assumption prevalent in our society that I challenge: Work is bad, and you should stop working as soon as you can. I believe there's dignity in work and that most people want to be useful to their communities. While you might be in a bad situation with your current job—it can be stressful to your health, you might be working too hard, you might be bored and ready for something new— retirement isn't the only fix for these problems. In fact, it may not even be feasible given your financial resources.

So let's focus on fixing the real problem, which is to make your work fulfilling and enjoyable in your later years. You don't necessarily need to make as much money or have the same drive and ambition that you did in your earlier years. Instead, the goal is to make enough money to supplement your other financial resources, to buy them time to grow (more on this in the next three steps), and to support the life that you want.

CHECKLIST OF ACTION STEPS FOR STEP 3: WORK AS LONG AS YOU CAN

- ❑ Think about how and where you might work during your retirement years. Discuss this with your spouse or partner, and friends or relatives.
- ❑ Review your contacts and current skill set. Are your contacts up to date? What about your skills? Are you in need of any training to get you up to speed?

HELPFUL RESOURCES

Books

- *What Color is Your Parachute - for Retirement*, by John Nelson and Richard Bolles
- *The Hard Times Guide to Retirement Security*, by Mark Miller
- *The Art of Happiness* and *The Art of Happiness at Work*, by the Dalai Lama and Dr. Howard Cutler
- *Aging Well*, by George Valliant
- *Successful Aging*, by John W. Rowe and Robert L. Kahn
- *Authentic Happiness*, by Martin Seligman
- *Project Renewment: The First Retirement Model for Career Women*, by Bernice Bratter and Helen Dennis

Websites

- www.aarp.org offers plenty of resources, but for our purposes here, once you're on the home page, click the tab on "Money" and then click the tab on "Work."
- www.encore.org, www.yourencore.com, and www.thetransitionnetwork.org all provide helpful resources on working in your later years.

STEP 4 Maximize Social Security Income by Delaying Benefits

One of the smartest things you can do to prepare for your *rest-of-life* is to make your Social Security income as large as possible by delaying benefits for as long as you can (but no later than age 70). The reason: For many people, Social Security benefits could be the only guaranteed lifetime income they'll receive. And for most people, Social Security replaces approximately 25% to 45% of their pay before retirement. By delaying benefits, you'll protect against these risks:

- Running out of money
- High inflation
- Stock market or interest rate fluctuations
- Death of a spouse

There are five really great advantages that Social Security income offers retirees. First, you'll receive a monthly income for life, no matter how long you live. Second, if you're married, Social Security income continues for your spouse after you die, no matter how long he or she lives. Third, your income is increased for inflation each year; most private pensions don't have a cost-of-living adjustment. Fourth, your Social Security benefits are not affected by what happens in the stock market. And finally, for many people, Social Security isn't subject to income taxes, or income taxes are reduced significantly. *There is no other benefit or financial asset that has this combination of powerful advantages.*

Basic Rules That Affect Your Income

Social Security's rules to determine benefits are very complex. Here are the most important factors, however, that impact the amount of your Social Security income:

- You need to have paid FICA taxes for at least 35 years to receive full benefits; otherwise, benefits are reduced.
- Starting benefits before your full retirement age (FRA) decreases your income. Note that Social Security also uses the term "normal retirement age" (NRA), which is the same as FRA. Age 62 is the earliest possible starting age.
- Starting benefits after your FRA will increase your income, at least until age 70. At that point, there are no further increases that come from delaying your income.
- Your spouse receives a separate income, based on the greater of his or her own earnings or 50% of your benefit (this latter amount is often referred to as the spousal benefit).
- Reductions for early retirement or increases for delayed retirement for your spouse's benefits are based on your spouse's age.

So just when is your Social Security full retirement age (FRA)? Here's the answer:

If you were born in	Then your FRA (or NRA) is
1937 or earlier	65 years
1938	65 years, 2 months
1939	65 years, 4 months
1940	65 years, 6 months
1941	65 years, 8 months
1942	65 years, 10 months
1943-1954	66 years
1955	66 years, 2 months
1956	66 years, 4 months
1957	66 years, 6 months
1958	66 years, 8 months
1959	66 years, 10 months
1960 or later	67 years

Estimating Your Benefits

The following tables will give you an idea of the amount of monthly Social Security income you can expect to receive. These figures were estimated using the calculators on the Social Security Administration's website and by making the following assumptions:

- Years of birth range from 1950 to 1965.
- Amounts shown are in 2014 dollars and do not reflect future adjustments for increases in wages or cost of living.
- The worker paid FICA taxes for 35 years to get the maximum benefit.
- The worker always made the salaries shown in the left column, adjusted for changes in average wages before 2014.

The first table is for people who have worked for most of their lives. If you're married and your spouse also worked a full career, then each of you would get a benefit based on your own wage history and your household income would be the sum of both incomes.

Table 4. Estimated Monthly Social Security Income for Workers

CURRENT SALARY ↓	AGE INCOME BEGINS →	AGE 62	AGE 65	FRA	AGE 70
$50,000		$1,140 to $1,175	$1,405 to $1,480	$1,510 to $1,715	$2,065 to $2,155
$75,000		$1,485 to $1,545	$1,860 to $1,945	$2,010 to $2,180	$2,690 to $2,790
$117,000 (maximum wages considered in 2014)		$1,895 to $1,990	$2,360 to $2,490	$2,595 to $2,735	$3,380 to $3,535

Here's the same table for a married worker, and assumes the spouse is the same age as the worker, did not work or worked sporadically, and receives the spousal benefit mentioned previously. The estimates shown are the sum of the worker's and spouse's benefits.

Table 5. Estimated Monthly Social Security Income for Married Couples Including Spousal Benefit

CURRENT SALARY ↓	AGE INCOME BEGINS →	AGE 62	AGE 65	FRA	AGE 70
$50,000		$1,665 to $1,720	$2,105 to $2,220	$2,265 to $2,570	$3,100 to $3,230
$75,000		$2,180 to $2,265	$2,795 to $2,915	$3,015 to $3,270	$4,035 to $4,185
$117,000 (maximum wages considered in 2014)		$2,780 to $2,915	$3,540 to $3,735	$3,890 to $4,100	$5,070 to $5,305

I've included these tables to give you a general idea of the amounts you might expect to receive from Social Security and to draw some basic conclusions, as follows:

- For many people, Social Security alone won't provide enough money for a comfortable retirement.
- There is a significant increase in income between starting your benefits at age 62, the earliest possible age, and delaying your benefits to your FRA or even age 70.

For most people, delaying the start of benefits is a good strategy, for two reasons:

- Social Security may be the only lifetime pension they receive.
- 401(k) balances and other resources may not generate sufficient lifetime earnings.

The best way to estimate *your* Social Security income is to go to the official website of the Social Security Administration (www.ssa.gov). The site offers calculators that use your own salary history to determine your benefits. The government also provides an online statement that shows an estimate of your benefits and your earnings history.

When Should *You* Start Benefits?

Is there any time it makes sense to start taking benefits as early as possible? Maybe. If you're in poor health, then the answer might be yes. Let me show you what I mean. The following table shows the total lifetime income for a single person earning $75,000 per year in 2014 for three different starting ages: age 62, FRA and age 70.

- The first row shows the initial annual Social Security income.
- The second row shows the total income over your life if you live to age 70 and then die. In this case, starting Social Security at age 62 is the best strategy, since the total lifetime income is the highest.
- The third row shows the total lifetime income if you live to age 80 and then die. In this case, starting Social Security at your FRA is the best strategy, because it provides the highest total lifetime income.
- The fourth row shows the total income if you live until age 90 and then die. In this case, starting Social Security at age 70 is the best strategy.

Table 6. Your Lifetime Social Security Income Depends on When You Start and How Long You Live

START SOCIAL SECURITY AT:	62 (EARLIEST)	66 (FRA)	70 (LATEST)
Initial annual income:	$18,540	$25,260	$33,480
Live to 70, total lifetime income:	***$148,320***	$101,040	$0
Live to 80, total lifetime income:	$333,720	***$353,640***	$334,800
Live to 90, total lifetime income:	$519,120	$606,240	***$669,600***
	Best strategy if you die at 70	Best strategy if you die at 80	Best strategy if you die at 90

Table 6 shows why it's good to have an estimate of how long you might live. Earlier, you saw in Tables 1 and 2 in the Introduction to this guidebook that the average age at death for Americans currently in their 50s and 60s is their mid-80s, which suggests that delaying Social Security benefits until FRA or beyond is the best strategy. Yet half of all Americans start Social Security at age 62, the earliest possible age with the lowest income, and 75% of Americans start before their FRA. It's my hope that the insights in this guidebook will help you make the best decision about the right time to start your Social Security benefits.

If you're worried about how you're going to make ends meet until you start receiving Social Security benefits, you may need to think about working while you still can in order to let your Social Security benefits grow. This can be part time—maybe just enough to make up for the Social Security funds you're delaying—or full time if you need more income. And working in your later years has other advantages that benefit your *rest-of-life*, as we discussed in Step 3.

What About Married Couples?

In most cases, delaying Social Security benefits works well for married couples. A very common situation is where the husband has been the primary wage earner and is older than his wife. Usually the husband dies before his wife, who would then receive a Social Security survivors benefit based on the husband's benefit. In this case, delaying the husband's Social Security benefit increases the wife's survivor income. Since poverty among elderly widows is a serious problem in our country, this strategy can significantly improve widows' financial security.

Here's one possible exception to the strategy to delay benefits. Suppose the wife is eligible for a Social Security benefit based on her *own* earnings and this benefit is much smaller than her husband's Social Security benefit. In this case, it might be best for her to start receiving *her* own benefits at an early age even though it might be best for her husband to delay *his* benefits. Determining when to start receiving benefits doesn't lend itself to easy rules of thumb; any decision you make regarding the age at which you'll begin receiving Social Security benefits should be thoroughly analyzed before you take action. Before you set your decision in stone, you should read more about the pros and cons of taking benefits early vs. holding off until your FRA or beyond, or work with a financial planner who's knowledgeable about strategies for maximizing the value of Social Security benefits.

How Working Affects Your Benefits

One last question you need to ask yourself is whether you should collect Social Security benefits while you work. The answer is, it all depends on your age. If you're over your full retirement age (FRA) and are still working, you can earn as much as possible from your job and still receive full Social Security benefits.

If you're under your FRA, however, then the Social Security Administration will apply the earnings test. If your earnings are at or under $15,480 during 2014 (the threshold increases every year), there's no reduction in your Social Security income. But if your earnings exceed this amount, then your income is reduced by $1 for every $2 of earnings over that amount. For example, suppose you're under your FRA and earn $17,480 during 2014—$2,000 over the threshold. Then your Social Security income will be reduced by $1,000.

There's a much more complicated test that applies just for the year in which you attain your FRA. For more information on this topic, visit the Social Security Administration's website at www.ssa.gov. At the top of the home page, search on the term "earnings test" to get more information.

A Few Last Points

I never cease to be amazed that financial planners and regular citizens alike disdainfully diss the Social Security program. I could retire right now if I had a nickel for every time I've heard "I'll never get Social Security benefits—it won't be around when I retire."

Let's face facts: Social Security is one of the most popular government programs around, and it's highly unlikely that our political leaders will eliminate it, particularly when baby boomers currently comprise the largest voting block.

Social Security does have funding challenges, however, *that can be solved* by making relatively modest adjustments. Bankruptcy of the program is not inevitable, as doomsayers would have you believe. But we need to support our leaders in making the choices that are necessary to keep Social Security viable and financially healthy for our lifetimes and beyond.

Determining the right time to start Social Security benefits is one of the key decisions you'll need to make regarding your retirement. Given current events and trends—the recent financial meltdown, improved longevity and the shift of responsibility for retirement adequacy from employers to individuals—now, more than ever, it's critical to make the most of your Social Security benefits.

CHECKLIST OF ACTION STEPS FOR STEP 4: MAXIMIZE SOCIAL SECURITY INCOME BY DELAYING THE START DATE

- ❑ Using the calculators on the Social Security Administration's website (www.ssa.gov), prepare estimates of your Social Security benefits at age 62, your FRA and age 70. Enter the results in **Worksheet #2: Estimating Your Total Retirement Income**, found in Section IV.
- ❑ Determine the best date to start your Social Security benefits, given your expected lifespan (and your spouse's lifespan, if you're married), how long you might work, and your need for income.
- ❑ Each year, check the online earnings history that's maintained by Social Security, to be sure it's accurate. If you find any mistakes in it, contact the Social Security Administration to have it corrected.

HELPFUL RESOURCES

- The Social Security Administration's website, www.ssa.gov, offers online calculators to help you determine the best date to start receiving benefits.
- You can also call the Social Security Administration at (800) 772-1213 to speak to a representative directly.
- Read *Social Security: The Inside Story*, by Andy Landis, or *Social Security for Dummies*, by Jon Peterson. Both are great sources on both Social Security and Medicare.
- Read *Innovative Strategies to Help Maximize Social Security Benefits*, by James Mahaney and Peter Carlson (www.prudential.com/media/managed/IB-InnovativeStrategies.pdf). You'll find good information regarding strategies for married couples and ideas for reducing your taxes.
- Helpful websites include www.socialsecuritychoices.com or www.socialsecuritytiming.com, both of which provide insights for married couples.

STEP 5 Be Prudent When Withdrawing Retirement Savings

When withdrawing your retirement savings, your number-one goal is this: Don't outlive your savings. Since most of us don't have any idea just when we'll die, you might think that's an impossible goal, but it's not.

Recent surveys have indicated that many current retirees are withdrawing funds from their savings much too quickly, with the inevitable result that they'll run out of money before they die. The problem is that many people "wing it" with regard to drawing down their retirement savings. Their 401(k) balances may look like a lot of money, so they withdraw what they need to cover their living expenses for the near future, without considering that their nest egg might need to last for a few decades.

By being careful with your withdrawals, you'll protect yourself against the following risks:

- Running out of money before you die
- Stock market or interest rate fluctuations that affect your retirement savings
- Death of a spouse, which could significantly reduce your retirement income

Instead of "winging it" I've got a better strategy for you, plus three methods to draw down and invest any type of retirement savings you have, whether it's a 401(k) plan, 403(b) plan, 457 plan, traditional or Roth IRA, or just an account that has no special tax features.

The Overriding Strategy

When it comes to your retirement savings, the most important thing you have to do is this: Don't consider your retirement assets as money you can spend in retirement. I know this sounds weird, but stay with me for a bit.

Let's say you have a few hundred thousand dollars or more, which seems like a lot of money, so you buy a new car, take expensive vacations or buy a vacation home—in other words, you live it up. But before you know it, your resources have dwindled significantly and you're worried about whether you'll have enough money to last.

Instead of letting your savings drain away, I'd like to offer an alternative: Consider your retirement savings to be a monthly paycheck generator. Then, spend no more than this paycheck. Most of us live paycheck to paycheck while we're working anyway, so let's not stop when we retire. To determine the size of your monthly retirement paycheck, use one of the methods described below, all of which minimize the chance of ruin (outliving your money).

Goals for Managing Your Retirement Savings

Your retirement income generator, or RIG for short, should produce a paycheck that increases periodically for inflation. This usually rules out portfolios invested exclusively in bonds and other fixed income investments. For most people, a portfolio invested in a mixture of stocks and bonds provides the desired balance between safety and protection against inflation. We'll talk about investing in more detail in Step 7. For now, let's get to the big challenge.

Your retirement income generator should provide funds that will last at least as long as you do. The three strategies described below are designed to survive economic downturns while generating a lifetime retirement income, no matter how long you live. And that's the big challenge, because you don't know how long that will be.

RIG # 1: Spend just your investment income. Spending just your interest and dividends virtually guarantees that you won't outlive your money. Interest and dividends aren't paid monthly, so you'll need to spread the income out appropriately. With a portfolio balanced between stocks and bonds, your annual income can range from 2% to 3% of your account balances; your actual rate will vary, depending on the specific asset allocation and the portfolio's emphasis on dividend-paying stocks.

This method works if your investment income is enough to cover your living expenses. If it's not, one of the other two methods described further ahead might work better for you. Also, it's the best method if leaving money to your children or charities is important to you. Of the three methods discussed in this step, this one has the highest chance of making your money last for your lifetime while giving you flexibility and access to your savings, but it provides the lowest amount of current income.

This method has two other advantages:

- You don't need to worry too much about the value the market places on your assets, as long as your interest and dividend stream is safe (which is an important goal that deserves your attention). Fluctuations in the dollar amount of the investment income from a diversified portfolio of stocks and bonds can be much less than the volatility of the underlying investments. If you just need the income from your investments, this can give you some peace of mind during times of market volatility.

- In case of an emergency, you can tap into your principal.

RIG # 2: Spend your principal cautiously. This method requires that you withdraw income and principal in a way that minimizes the likelihood that you'll outlive the principal. One rule of thumb to make this happen is to calculate 4% of your retirement savings that are remaining at the beginning of each year, then divide by 12 to determine your monthly paycheck. Of course, there's still a chance you'll outlive your resources, but the odds are low—roughly one out of 10. If you're in your seventies (as opposed to your late fifties or sixties), you might be able to increase your withdrawal percentage to 5% and still have enough principal to continue generating enough income.

There are online calculators that can help you determine the odds of ruin with various withdrawal strategies. I like the Retirement Income Calculator at www.troweprice.com. If you use such a calculator, I suggest that you focus on the strategies that give you very high odds of success—I prefer 90% (more on this subject in Section III).

This second method is designed to help you withstand the worst scenario—a significant drop in the value of your investments early in your retirement (as happened in the fall of 2008). If this scenario happens, using this method means you'll have sufficient assets invested when the market bounces back (as it typically has in the past). If you're withdrawing too much principal during a market downturn, you might not have enough invested assets to recover.

While no one wants to encounter a "worst case" scenario, it's smart to employ strategies that will help you survive one. We've certainly learned this lesson the hard way with the 2008-2009 stock market crash. And if the worst case doesn't happen and your portfolio appreciates, then you can enjoy future increases in your retirement income when you apply the 4% or 5% rate to a higher asset value.

This method works best if you need more income than just interest and dividends, and if leaving money to children or charities isn't as important as maximizing your retirement income. You also have the flexibility to tap into your principal, if an emergency arises.

RIG #3: Buy an immediate annuity. Don't confuse immediate annuities with deferred annuities, which are investment vehicles that can have high expenses. With an immediate annuity, you give a lump sum of money to an insurance company and they promise to pay a monthly income for life. It's really a do-it-yourself pension.

When it comes to annuities, I prefer this straightforward type that simply pays you a fixed amount for the rest of your life. These annuities typically have the lowest transaction and commission costs. Acceptable variations include annuities that have specified increases built in for inflation and annuities that continue income to a spouse or beneficiary in case you die first. Both of these variations cost more, although the extra price can be worth it. Be careful with annuities that have bells and whistles with high costs and commissions, such as variable annuities that invest in the stock market but have a cap on market losses.

If you buy an annuity with a fixed monthly income, there's no inflation protection. For this reason, you may want to invest just a portion of your retirement savings in an annuity—say one-third to one-half. Then invest the remainder of your portfolio in stocks and other assets that provide inflation protection, and use one of the first two methods to generate additional income.

How much will you get from this type of annuity? That depends on a number of factors:

- Your age and sex at the time you buy the annuity
- Whether you cover a beneficiary
- The safety of the insurance company
- Interest rates at the time you buy the annuity

It's important to choose a highly rated insurance company from which to buy the annuity. There's no federal protection for annuities, like there is for bank savings accounts with FDIC insurance. However, most states have insurance guaranty associations, and it's important to learn about their limits. Go to the website for the insurance guaranty association in your state to learn more.

You can go online to both Moody's Investors Service (www.moodys.com) and Standard & Poor's (www.standardandpoors.com) to check the ratings on an insurance company's strength. The safest approach is to buy from a company with one of the four highest ratings. For Moody's, this would be Aaa, Aa1, Aa2 and Aa3. And for Standard & Poor's, you'd want to look for a rating of AAA , AA+, AA or AA-.

So how do you buy an immediate annuity? You can use an online service, such as www.immediateannuities.com or www.incomesolutions.com, both of which have educational information including summaries of state insurance guaranty associations. Or you can contact an insurance broker, who will shop your annuity among several insurance companies to get the best deal. Finally, you could contact a financial planner or investment advisor. But be careful with these last two options! Always ask how much their commission is and whether they shop for the best deal among several insurance companies.

An immediate annuity typically has two disadvantages the first two methods don't have: You won't be able to leave money to children or charities, and you can't dip into your principal if an emergency arises. However, an annuity has one great feature that the other two methods don't have: You don't need to manage your money. This might be especially helpful when you get to your eighties or nineties and might not be as sharp as you used to be.

One Example, Three Ways

Suppose you've saved $100,000 for retirement. Let's compare how much annual lifetime income the three methods I just described will generate.

RIG #1: Spend just the investment income: Assuming the dividend and interest rate of your assets is 3% per year, then 3% of $100,000 is $3,000 per year.

RIG #2: Spend principal cautiously: At a 4% drawdown rate, 4% of $100,000 is $4,000 per year. A 5% drawdown rate would produce an annual income of $5,000 per year.

RIG #3: Invest in an immediate annuity: In January, 2014, www.incomesolutions.com showed that $100,000 would buy a 65-year-old man a fixed annual income of about $7,070. A 65-year-old woman would receive about $6,740; a married couple (both age 65) would receive about $5,950 per year until the last person dies.

Buying an immediate annuity provides a higher income than the first two methods, so why wouldn't you put all your money in an annuity? Remember that the annual income from an annuity is usually fixed, while your income under the first two methods should increase with favorable investment returns. There are other reasons, too, as discussed below.

Income Diversification

You're probably familiar with investment diversification, where you spread your investments across different types of assets and use more than just a few securities. For our purposes, an important refinement of this concept is income diversification, where you'd use two or more methods of generating retirement income. This way, you can balance the advantages and disadvantages of each method.

For example, it's not recommended that you put all your money in an immediate fixed annuity since you won't have money available for emergencies and you won't have protection against inflation. The best choice is to deploy just a portion of your portfolio to an annuity, say one-third to one-half, and use one of the first two withdrawal methods for the rest of your portfolio.

And the appropriate withdrawal method can change as you age. Here's one good way to shift these strategies over your lifetime. In Phase 1 of your retirement (as described in Step 3), when you're in your "early" retirement years—your late sixties and early seventies—use the first method and live on your investment income. If this doesn't provide enough income, then work part time while you still can. Working part time also means you'll have a fallback source of income if there's a significant downturn in your portfolio.

Then wait until Phase 2—your mid-seventies or later—to begin drawing principal and/or buying an annuity. This might coincide with when you stop working altogether. With an annuity, you'll get a better rate for waiting; consider it to be "insurance" in case you live to 100.

Traps for the Unwary

One bad choice I've seen people make again and again is to spend significant amounts of their retirement funds in their "early" retirement years and rationalize it by thinking they'll spend less money on travel and recreation in their later years. This is risky business! While it's true that travel and recreation expenses might decrease, medical expenses are likely to increase in your later years and can easily exceed the money you would have spent on travel and recreation. This is yet another reason why it's smart to be prudent in your early retirement years and supplement your retirement income with wage income.

Here's one more potential snag: If your money is in a 401(k), 403(b) or 457 plan, or a traditional IRA, pay attention to the minimum distribution rules (Roth IRAs aren't subject to these rules). Once you reach age 70-1/2, the IRS requires you to withdraw minimum amounts from these accounts, and they apply significant penalties if you don't. This doesn't mean you have to *spend* the money; instead, you can withdraw the money and put it in a taxable investment account. Many of the websites in the Resources section at the end of this step have details on these rules.

As you can see, drawing down your retirement savings isn't a "one size fits all" exercise. It's part art, part science. It takes patience, skill and understanding of the issues. Knowing what would be best for you can also help you decide when you can retire: If using these methods doesn't generate enough income, then you might decide to continue working for awhile. Or, you may want to revisit your living expenses, and look for ways to manage them to gain your retirement freedom. See Step 8 for more details.

Worksheet #3: Estimating Income from Savings/401(k) Plans in Section IV offers an easy way to project your account balances and estimate the resulting "paycheck" that your balances will generate. Alternatively, you can use some of the websites listed below in the Resources section to determine your estimated retirement income.

It's well worth your time to learn about all the methods and figure out which combination works best for you. The last thing you want to do is spend too much money in your sixties and seventies, and then need to go back to work in your eighties because you've run out of money. Instead, you want to feel confident that you can afford to live to see your 90s—and maybe even 100!

CHECKLIST OF ACTION STEPS FOR STEP 5: BE PRUDENT WHEN WITHDRAWING RETIREMENT SAVINGS

- ❑ Become familiar with the three methods of withdrawing funds from your savings, and think about which methods might work best for your circumstances.

- ❑ Project your accounts to your desired retirement ages and your estimated annual retirement income, using **Worksheet #3: Estimating Income from Savings/401(k) Plans**. Enter the results in **Worksheet #2: Estimating Your Total Retirement Income.** You can refine your analyses with online calculators or spreadsheets—see Section III for more insights.

HELPFUL RESOURCES

Books and Publications

- *Money for Life: Turn Your IRA and 401(k) Into a Lifetime Retirement Paycheck,* by Steve Vernon
- *Live Long & Prosper: Invest in Your Happiness, Health and Wealth for Retirement and Beyond*, by Steve Vernon
- *Don't Run with Your Retirement Money*, by The Actuarial Foundation and Women's Institute for a Secure Retirement (WISER). For a downloadable copy, visit www.actuarialfoundation.org/consumer/dont-run.htm
- *Making Your Money Last for a Lifetime: What You Need to Know About Annuities*, by The Actuarial Foundation. For a downloadable copy, visit www.actuarialfoundation.org/publications/wiser_annuities.shtml

Websites

- www.actuarialfoundation.org
- www.incomesolutions.com
- www.immediateannuities.com
- www.fidelity.com
- www.wiser.org
- howmuchcaniaffordtospendinretirement.webs.com
- www.moneyforlifeguideonline.com
- http://wpfau.blogspot.com
- www.morningstar.com
- www.troweprice.com
- www.vanguard.com

STEP 6 Maximize Income From Traditional Pension Plans

If you'll be getting a significant lifetime income from a traditional pension plan (a.k.a. a defined benefit plan) from your employer, count yourself lucky. You stand the best chance of enjoying a traditional retirement, and the odds are good that you won't outlast your financial resources. In this case, the smartest thing you can do is to maximize this lifetime income by delaying your benefits until they've reached their maximum. This is usually the "normal retirement age" under the plan, which is often age 65 but sometimes earlier.

Why should you maximize your pension income? Doing so helps protect against these risks:

- Running out of money
- Stock market or interest rate fluctuations
- Death of a spouse

There are several factors that can affect the amount of your monthly retirement income from a pension. Most plans use your years of service to calculate benefits, so the longer you work, the larger your pension will be. Most plans also provide reductions for retirement before the normal retirement age, so delaying retirement until the normal retirement age results in the largest benefit. And some plans base the benefit on your compensation, so the larger your pay, the larger your retirement income will be.

The great thing about getting income from a traditional pension plan is that you have very few decisions to make. The most important is probably whether you want to elect to continue part or all of your monthly income to your spouse after you die (a joint and survivor election). This option usually reduces your initial monthly income, to pay for this "life insurance," but most married people elect this type of protection. Beware of the "pass on the joint and survivor election and buy life insurance instead" strategy that some life insurance agents advocate. I've seen analyses that supposedly show this is a better financial strategy, but you and your spouse have to die at just the right times to make it work and that rarely happens.

After you make your election, the money just comes in the mail or is deposited electronically each month in your bank account. You don't have to make decisions regarding investing or drawing down your savings; you'll really appreciate this when you get older and are less able to manage your finances.

Some plans offer a lump sum option in lieu of a monthly income. If you have this choice, carefully investigate the pros and cons. For many people, taking the lump sum can be the wrong choice; it only makes sense if you're not healthy, or if you think the plan is underfunded, the sponsor might go bankrupt, and your benefit is greater than guarantees by the Pension Benefit Guaranty Corporation (PBGC, which is like the FDIC for pensions). My website (www.restoflife.com) has an article that goes into details on the pros and cons of lump sums from pension plans, including checklists for the circumstances when each choice might be best. See *Should You Take a Lump Sum from Your Pension Plan?* on the "Newsletters and Articles" page on www.restoflife.com.

Note that arguments against a lump sum payment as described above apply only to *tax-qualified* pension plans that have invested assets in a trust fund that is protected from creditors in case of bankruptcy—the kind of pension plan that most people participate in. It's a different story for *nonqualified* plans that are only for highly paid employees or executives; these plans typically don't have assets in a trust fund that is protected from creditors, so you need to be concerned with the ability of the plan sponsor to pay your benefits for the rest of your life. As a result, the case for taking a lump sum from a *nonqualified* plan is much stronger than the case for taking a lump sum from a *tax-qualified* pension plan.

If you participate in a traditional pension plan, here are a few more things you should understand:

- Be aware of any thresholds that would increase your benefits. For instance, a plan might provide full benefits at 30 years of service in the plan, even if you retire before the normal retirement age.
- If you work part time, be aware of how the plan reflects your service and compensation. You don't want working part time to reduce your ultimate pension. Usually this doesn't happen, but it's a good idea to check.
- Be sure the plan administrator has accurate information about your service time and compensation.
- If you decide to stop working before the normal retirement age and there's a reduction for early retirement, find out if your plan allows you to delay benefit commencement until the normal retirement age, which would eliminate the early retirement reduction. This might be a smart thing to do if the early retirement reduction is large, say 5% or more for each year you retire early.

You can learn more about your defined benefit plan from the Summary Plan Description (SPD) that your employer publishes. Many plans also provide estimates of your income through online calculators. You can also make a request to your human resources department or the plan administrator. It might take some patience and persistence, particularly with online calculators. But hang in there and ask questions if you're confused. It's smart to take the time and effort to learn how to get the most from this valuable benefit.

CHECKLIST OF ACTION STEPS FOR STEP 6: MAXIMIZE INCOME FROM TRADITIONAL PENSION PLANS

- ❑ Estimate your income at your desired retirement ages. To do this, use the online calculator available from your employer, if applicable. If one isn't available, ask your human resources department or plan administrator for an estimate. Enter the results in **Worksheet #2: Estimating Your Total Retirement Income** in Section IV.

- ❑ If your plan offers a lump sum payment in lieu of the monthly pension, become familiar with the pros and cons of this decision and decide which option is appropriate for your circumstances. Don't be influenced by what your friends are doing.

HELPFUL RESOURCES

- *Live Long & Prosper: Invest in Your Happiness, Health and Wealth for Retirement and Beyond*, by Steve Vernon
- *Should You Take a Lump Sum Payment from Your Pension Plan? A Trap for the Unwary*, by Steve Vernon. See the "Newsletters and Articles" page on www.restoflife.com to access this article.

STEP 7 Manage Your Investment Risk and Invest for Income

There are many different perspectives on investing for retirement. Here I'll share my philosophy and strategies, which have been influenced by studying the effects of the stock market crash of 2008-2009 and prior downturns. It turns out that the lessons taught to me by my grandfather, who was a stockbroker in the Great Depression, apply very well to the most recent meltdown—and most likely will continue to apply as we all attempt to protect ourselves from future meltdowns. The ideas aren't new—they are classic investment strategies.

If you're within ten years of retirement or are already retired, it's critical to strike a balance between protecting against two potentially significant risks: market losses and inflation. Here are two investing strategies that address this goal:

1. Manage your risks through asset allocation, and
2. Invest for income.

Following these strategies also protects against the critical risk of outliving your savings.

So now that you know what you *should* do, how do you begin? Let's start by reviewing my "Recession-Proof Investment Strategies." It has three parts that help you find the right balance of growth for the long run but protects against economic downturns. Here's how it works:

1. Diversify across asset classes to mitigate the impact of a specific type of economic downturn (i.e. don't have all your eggs in one basket).
2. Know your limits for investment risk and your investing skills, and invest accordingly.

3. As you approach your retirement years, shift to investing for income.

I'll go into more detail on these strategies in the following pages. But before you can actually put your money to work for you, you've got to take two "Investment Action Steps." These two pre-investing steps will help you make the right choices when it comes to investing your retirement savings:

1. Understand investment basics and asset classes.
2. Decide what type of investor you are by evaluating your risk tolerance and financial knowledge.

Understanding Investment Basics and Asset Classes

When it comes to investing, there are two rules you need to remember, no matter how much you have to invest or what type of investments you plan to use:

1. **There is no such thing as a "risk free" investment.** All investments entail some form of risk, such as market risk, interest rate risk or inflation.
2. **Past performance does not necessarily predict future performance.** However, we *can* gain valuable insights by analyzing historical trends; we just need to keep our eye on the future to see how it might be different from the past.

To some degree or another, every investor wants three things out of an investment: (1) safety, (2) income and (3) growth. Safety is the trait that makes you think "Please, just don't let it go down." Income means to generate money, continuously. And growth is to be worth more in the future than now.

Certain asset classes emphasize each of these traits. Stocks are often associated with growth, bonds with income, and cash or cash equivalents with safety. However, dividend-paying stocks and certain types of real estate can provide income with potential for growth, and these are investments we'll explore later.

There are also different risks associated with each asset class. For stocks, it's the short-term market volatility you'll need to be concerned with. For bonds, it's the interest rate you have to worry about. And for cash or cash equivalents, such as savings accounts, money market funds and CDs, you need to take long-term inflation into account.

I won't go into details here describing these types of investments, because you probably have very good educational materials at hand through your 401(k) plans at work. If you don't have access to any educational resources, then check out some of the publications and websites listed in the Resources section at the end of this step. By the way, whenever I say "401(k) plans," you should assume I also mean 403(b) saving plans at nonprofits, 457 saving plans at government employers, IRAs, and any other type of retirement savings vehicle.

Now let's review some historical statistics on the stock market to help us get some perspective.

Insights From History

Chart 1 below shows annual stock returns since 1926, using the S&P 500 index. Note that 2008 was the second worst year on record.

Chart 1. Annual Stock Returns Since 1926

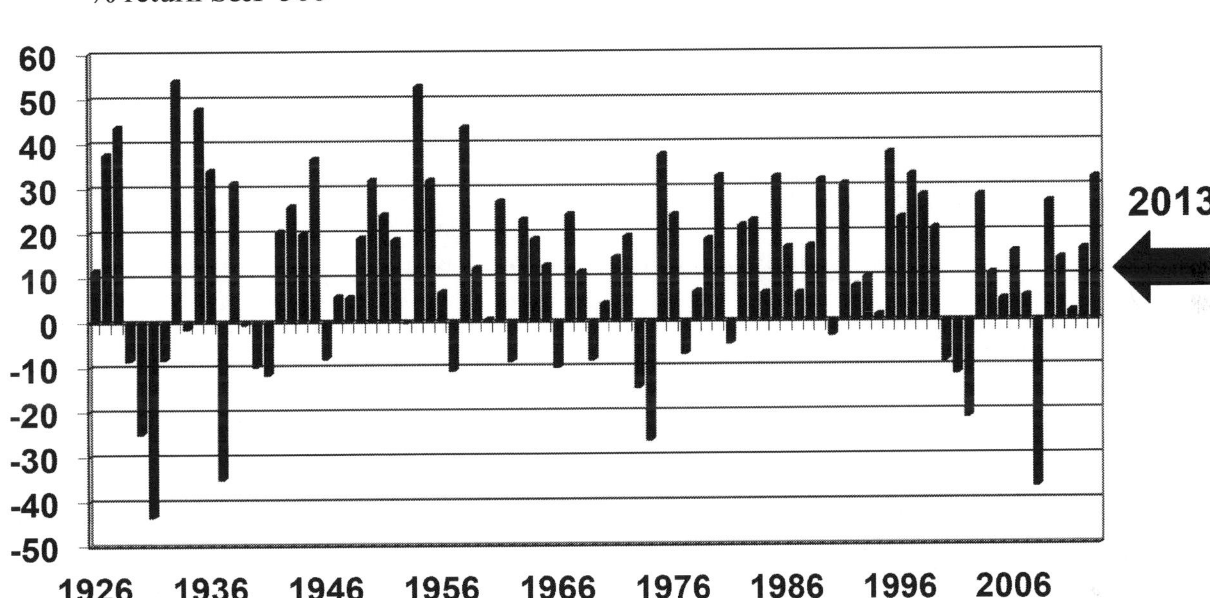

The actual experience in 2008 and 2009 illustrates the limitations of looking just at annual returns. The market continued to decline significantly in early 2009, but then came roaring back and resulted in a net return in 2009 of about 26.5%.

Chart 1 also shows what I call the "stock market double-double." If you look at the chart again, you'll see that there are approximately twice as many "up" years as "down" years, and the "up" bars go up about twice as high as the "down" bars go down. By the end of 2013, the stock market had completely recovered from its big drop in 2008-2009. People who stayed invested and didn't panic by selling at the market bottom were rewarded for their patience.

How long might you need to wait? Table 7 below shows the length of time that it took the market to recover from prior severe downturns (defined as a drop of 20% or more in the S&P 500 index). The first column shows how long the downturn was—from the high to the low in the S&P index— with the second column showing the exact percentage of the loss. The third column shows how long it took for the market to go from the low back to the previous high; this was the time investors had to wait for recovery.

Table 7. Months to Recover From Prior Stock Market Crashes

Length of downturn	Percent loss	Months to recovery
1929 – 34 months	-83.4%	151 months
1946 – 6 months	-21.8%	35 months
1962 – 6 months	-22.3%	10 months
1968 – 19 months	-29.3%	9 months
1973 – 21 months	-42.6%	21 months
1987 – 3 months	-29.5%	18 months
2000 – 25 months	-48.9%	54 months

In the worst case—back in the Great Depression—it took the market more than 12 years to recover. But if you average the recovery periods, it works out to about three-and-a-half years. If you're in your 50s, 60s or 70s now, you'll most likely still be alive in three-and-a-half years—even in 12 years. So you have the time to wait, particularly if you have other sources of financial security as advocated in the other steps in this guidebook.

The Importance of Diversification

Because of the risks mentioned above, it's important that you diversify your investments to reduce your overall risk. You'll want to diversify two ways:

1. *Across* asset classes
2. *Within* asset classes

When you diversify *across* asset classes, you mitigate the risk of different types of economic challenges. To diversify across asset classes, you'll want to invest in a mix of stocks, bonds, real estate and cash, because each behaves differently in diverse economic climates. Some mutual funds, such as target retirement date, balanced or asset allocation funds, provide diversification across asset classes.

The downward trends in the stock market in 2008 provided a tough lesson on why you should diversify across asset classes. Let's look at the 2008 returns of various Vanguard mutual funds that have different asset allocations to see why diversifying is a good objective.

Table 8. 2008 Returns of Various Vanguard Mutual Funds

Fund	2008 annual return
GNMA (100% government bonds)	7.22%
Treasury money market	2.10%
Wellesley Income (2/3 bonds, 1/3 stocks)	-9.84%
Wellington (1/3 bonds, 2/3 stocks)	-22.30%
S&P 500 fund (100% stocks)	-37.02%
REIT index	-37.05%
FTSE All World ex-US index	-44.09%

I selected these particular Vanguard funds because they're widely used and their return history is ready available on the internet.

The year 2008 represents a possible "worst case scenario" for potential future losses in the stock market. But when you want to decide how much risk you can tolerate, don't look at percentages. Instead, ask how much money you can afford to lose. For instance, suppose you had invested $100,000 in each of the above funds at the beginning of 2008. Could you afford to lose the following amounts?

Table 9. 2008 Losses on $100,000 Invested with Various Vanguard Funds

Fund	2008 loss
Wellesley Income (2/3 bonds, 1/3 stocks)	-$9,840
Wellington (1/3 bonds, 2/3 stocks)	-$22,300
S&P 500 fund (100% stocks)	-$37,020
REIT index	-$37,050
FTSE All World ex-US index	-$44,090

It's my opinion that people in their 50s and beyond should consider having no more than two-thirds of their money invested in the stock market, to protect against market losses, and no less than one-third in the stock market, to protect against future inflation. This range is represented by the Wellington fund (2/3 in the stock market) with a 2008 loss of $22,300, and the Wellesley fund (a little more than 1/3 in the stock market) with a 2008 loss of $9,840. While these losses are definitely hard to bear, most people can recover from such losses, particularly if they've followed the other steps in this guidebook.

Unfortunately, before the market losses of 2008, many people chased high returns and had high allocations to stocks. When warned about the risks, they didn't think that stocks could drop as far as they did. As you can see from Table 9, such investors experienced large dollar losses. Stop and think about how much money you can tolerate to lose; this will help you work out the asset allocation that's right for you.

This reminds me of some smart advice I got from my stockbroker grandfather: Invest amounts that you *can't* afford to lose in bonds and cash, whereas invest in stocks only the dollar amounts you *can* afford to lose 50% or more of. And when you're considering how much you can afford to lose, consider *all* your financial resources, such as Social Security, pensions or annuities, your house, etc.

Investing for retirement also requires the nerves and patience to ride out downturns, and the 2008-2009 downturn is providing a good lesson on why this is important. Let's take a look at Table 10, which repeats Table 9, but I've added the gains through the end of 2013.

Table 10. 2008 Losses and 2009-2013 Gains on $100,000 Invested at the Beginning of 2008 with Various Vanguard Funds

Fund	2008 loss	2009-2013 gain	Net gain/loss
Wellesley Income (2/3 bonds, 1/3 stocks)	-$9,840	$62,330	$52,490
Wellington (1/3 bonds, 2/3 stocks)	-$22,300	$69.653	$47,353
S&P 500 fund (100% stocks)	-$37,020	$79,992	$42,902
REIT index	-$37,050	$73,551	$36,501
FTSE All World ex-US index	-$44,090	$44,399	$309

In just five years, the market has rewarded our patience and has come back. All of the funds have recovered all of their losses and much more, except for the FTSE All World ex-US index fund, which has barely broken even.

Now let's talk about diversifying *within* asset classes. When you do that, you'll invest in multiple securities in order to mitigate the risk of poor performance of one particular stock or bond. A stock mutual fund, for instance, invests in the stocks of many companies, and a mutual fund for REITs (real estate investment trust) invests in many pooled real estate trusts.

Many people got burned when they invested a large part of their 401(k) savings in their own company stock, and the stock later tanked or became worthless. They could have avoided this fate by diversifying their hard-earned savings.

By the way, your own home is a significant investment in real estate, and in most cases, I think it's a good idea to own a home that is within your means and meets your living needs. It's even better if you can pay off the mortgage early in your retirement years, and particularly before you retire completely.

Usually I don't count your home as a retirement investment; instead, I consider it as a way to manage your living expenses, which is a different goal. Of course, you can sell your home to realize a profit, but recent declines in real estate values have illustrated the risk of this strategy. Most of the time, your own home won't generate income during your retirement years to cover your ordinary living expenses. The one possible exception—and it's a good one for some people—is to rent out a room or two to a boarder while you're still living there. Yes, you could get a reverse mortgage or home equity loan, but I think it's a mistake to use these to pay for ordinary living expenses while you could still work. As mentioned previously in Step 2, I prefer that you hold reverse mortgages and home equity loans in reserve until you desperately need the money, for instance, to pay for long-term care expenses.

What Type of Investor Are You?

As you're evaluating how you should invest, you must also look at the type of investor you are. A conservative investor is concerned with safety above all else; a typical conservative asset allocation would have no more than one-third of assets in stocks with the rest in bonds. A moderate investor is willing to take on a little more risk—his or her typical asset allocation would have one-third to two-thirds of assets in stocks with the rest in bonds. And an aggressive investor accepts quite a bit of risk, so he or she might invest two-thirds or more of their assets in stocks with the balance in bonds.

There are scores of statistics that examine rates of return over long periods of time; such studies have examined every 10-year period, every 20-year period, and so on. For most 10- and 20-year periods, portfolios with higher allocations to stocks have had higher returns than bonds and cash investments. This has been the traditional reason for significant allocations to stocks for long-term investments, such as retirement savings.

Of course, there have been times when portfolios with higher allocations to stocks have had worse returns compared to those invested in bonds and stocks—and the stock market crash in 2008 provided one of those "occasional" times. For the 10-year periods ending on December 31, 2008 and December 31, 2009, returns on stocks were negative, and stocks lagged behind all other investments. You might take some comfort that this has happened before and the stock market recovered to go on to new highs.

So the key question is this: Will the recent stock market recovery last? Will the U.S. economy recover? I don't have a crystal ball that's reliable, and neither does anybody else. So I'm hedging my bets: I'll continue investing in stocks for the potential of long-term growth. However, I'll limit my investments in stocks so that if they do poorly, it won't ruin me. And I'll have other resources to sustain me as advocated elsewhere in this book.

The Recession-Proof Investment Strategies Revisited

Now that you're a little more familiar with the basics of investing, let's revisit the three-part Recession-Proof Investment Strategies described at the beginning of this chapter.

Strategy #1: Diversify across asset classes to mitigate the impact of a specific type of economic downturn. Manage your risk through an allocation between stocks, bonds, real estate and cash investments that is appropriate for you. If you've decided which type of investor you are—conservative, moderate or aggressive—you've got a good start for developing guidelines to allocate your assets between these investments.

While you're refining your asset allocation decision, consider your entire situation in your retirement years. A substantial income from a defined benefit plan or annuity and/or low living expenses, such as a paid-off mortgage, might suggest a higher toleration for volatility and higher allocation to stocks. In this case, your income can still cover your living expenses even if the stock market goes down. But a small income stream from a pension or annuity, or having only enough funds to barely cover your essential living expenses, might suggest a lower allocation to stocks because you can't tolerate the volatility. In this case, a stock market decline could jeopardize your $I > E$ relationship.

One option to consider is to take a chunk of your allocation to stocks and put it in real estate or international stocks, if you believe they provide additional diversification and future growth opportunities. These types of investments did well leading up to the 2008-2009 stock market crash, though they got hammered just like everything else. I still believe in diversifying with these investments, in spite of their experience in 2008-2009. However, I limit my exposure to no more than 10% of my total portfolio in each of these types of investments with the balance of my stock allocation going to U.S. stocks. If you're interested in investing in real estate and international stocks, then I'd suggest you invest in mutual funds and REITs since they provide both diversification and professional management. Owning individual properties in investment real estate is like running a small business; you should only do that if you have the time and necessary skills to manage them well.

Strategy #2: Know your limits and invest accordingly. Most people don't have the time or expertise to buy and sell individual stocks, bonds and real estate. If this is you, my best advice is to keep it simple and avoid common mistakes. Invest in time-tested assets: highly rated no-load mutual funds in stocks and bonds, FDIC-insured bank accounts, money market funds and possibly real estate through mutual funds of REITs.

So just where should you invest? First, in most cases, it pays to maximize your contributions to your 401(k) plan. The plan sponsor does the fund shopping for you and makes saving easy through payroll deductions. In a few instances, particularly with small employers, large fees can be charged to your account, so it's a good idea to investigate before you invest.

Many 401(k) plans provide "one decision" funds called target retirement date funds or balanced funds. These are one of the best financial innovations in recent years: You decide your risk tolerance and asset allocation, then choose the fund that's the best match.

Let me elaborate a little on these types of funds, since they have significant differences.

- "Balanced funds" typically have a stated allocation between stocks, bonds, cash and sometimes real estate, and they usually stick to the target allocation.
- "Asset allocation funds" can vary the allocation between various types of investments, depending on the investment manager's outlook on the economy. If the manager has a positive outlook regarding stocks, money is shifted into stocks. If the manager has a bearish outlook on stocks, money is shifted into bonds or cash.
- "Target retirement date funds" or "lifestyle funds" pick an asset allocation that the investment manager considers appropriate *today* for a given *future* retirement date, and then as the date approaches, they reduce the risk of market volatility by shifting assets from stocks to bonds.

Warning: Some people who invested in target retirement date funds were disappointed when their funds lost money in 2008. Even funds with a 2010 target retirement date lost money. It's not uncommon for 2010 target date funds to currently have about 50% of their assets invested in stocks, since the investment managers believe that people close to or in retirement should still have significant amounts invested in the stock market. It's also not uncommon for a 2020 retirement date fund to currently invest more than two-thirds of its assets in stocks. Also keep in mind that the various mutual fund families can have different opinions on the appropriate asset allocation for a specific retirement date.

If you're considering a target retirement date fund, don't blindly decide on your retirement date and then pick the corresponding target retirement date fund. It's much better to look at the fund's specific asset allocation between stocks, bonds, cash, and real estate (if applicable), and decide if that allocation is right for you. Selecting a fund based on its asset allocation might even result in you selecting a target retirement date fund with a stated retirement date that is different from your own retirement date—that's OK. It definitely pays to "look under the hood" of target retirement date funds and not just rely on a number on the calendar!

For any money you have to invest in addition to your 401(k) contributions, consider no-load mutual fund families that offer a good lineup of highly rated funds and robust online education and planning tools. Good places to start looking are Fidelity Investments, T. Rowe Price and Vanguard, which all have a variety of funds with good track records, including the "one choice" funds mentioned previously, such as balanced or target date funds. They also have money market funds and mutual funds that invest in international stocks and REITs. They have extensive online and telephone services and lower expenses than average. You can visit www.morningstar.com for more information and ratings on most mutual funds.

For any additional funds you have that you'd like to use for cash investments, try money market funds and FDIC-insured CDs or savings accounts at banks, but shop around as rates can change. If you want to buy an immediate annuity, as described in Step 5, visit www.immediateannuities.com or www.incomesolutions.com for more information and the ability to shop online among different insurance companies.

So that's what you *should* look into. But what about investment vehicles or sources you should avoid? Here are a few you should be wary of:

- **Whole life insurance (a.k.a. universal life or variable universal life).** These products mix protection (insurance) with investing. Unfortunately, the premiums are usually high and the returns can be mediocre. If you need insurance, it's usually best to buy term insurance—which has much lower premiums—and invest the difference elsewhere.
- **Tax-deferred annuities (TDAs) with high expenses.** The only reason to consider TDAs is if you're in a high tax bracket, because this product defers taxation on investment income. However, you should only use TDAs after maxing out contributions to your 401(k) plan. Even then, if you're in a high tax bracket, you may be better off with investments with minimal taxes on investment earnings, such as municipal bonds or index funds. If you still want a TDA, then pick one with a good investment track record and low expenses, such as those offered by Fidelity, T. Rowe Price or Vanguard.
- **Most stockbrokers who buy and sell individual stocks and bonds for you, unless you have $500,000 or more to invest.** It's hard to find a good advisor who will work with "small" amounts to invest. Instead, mutual funds and other commingled investments provide professional management to investors with "small" amounts.

- **Financial advisors who recommend load mutual funds.** There's been no measurable difference in the overall investment performance of load vs. no-load funds, so why pay the up-front fee?
- **Anybody who makes unrealistic promises about investment returns.** Instead, learn what's realistic for different types of investments. Over long periods of time, annual stock returns have averaged from 9% to 10%. Bonds and other fixed income investments have earned in the 4% to 7% range, depending on the issuer and maturity period. If somebody "guarantees" or implies they can achieve much higher returns, take your money and run! If something seems too good to be true, most likely it is.
- **Tax shelters.** These only make sense for people with a lot of money, and even then, they're difficult to compare and analyze.
- **"Hot" stock tips.** Take the time to investigate your investments. Don't jump at tips you hear about at the beauty salon or hardware store; do your "tipsters" look like professional financial advisors?
- **Your brother-in-law or "advisors" you meet in social situations or who are recommended by family or friends,** unless they have good credentials and a good track record. In other words, check them out just as you would anybody else. A common type of fraud is called affinity fraud, where financial criminals are masters at getting recommended by friends and family members. In 2008, Bernie Madoff provided the latest example of affinity fraud. Well-known celebrities got taken just because their buddies recommended him and Madoff promised them high returns. As a result, Madoff "made off" with their money. Remember: Know what's realistic!

All the above situations aren't necessarily bad, but there's enough potential for poor outcomes that you should investigate them very carefully. If you don't have the time or expertise, it may be best to avoid them altogether and stick with the "tried and true."

Strategy #3: As you approach your retirement years, shift to investing for income. Fluctuations in the dollar amounts of dividend and interest income from diversified portfolios of stocks, bonds and real estate have been much lower than fluctuations in the value of the underlying investments. So if you use just your investment income for living expenses, you're partially insulated from market fluctuations. You don't care if your stocks have dropped as long as the dividends keep coming in, and you don't care what you could sell the real estate for as long as rental income continues. Granted, companies will cut dividends if they hit bad times, rental income can and will dip during a recession, and interest rates can drop. But if you've diversified your investment income, if you have other sources of income as advocated by this guidebook and if you're managing your living expenses, you can survive these temporary reductions in investment income.

This strategy has more advantages. If you live on just the investment income, as described in Step 5, you have a disciplined approach to both investing and withdrawing from savings which virtually guarantees that you won't outlive your savings. And for your investments outside of a 401(k) plan, you can take advantage of a lower federal income tax on qualified dividends—15%—compared to ordinary income, which is taxed at rates of up to 35%.

If you don't invest for income and you need to withdraw money periodically for living expenses, then you'll constantly be selling investments. This creates some challenges: Eventually you'll be forced to sell when the market is down, or you'll always be wondering whether it is a good time to sell your investments. This can be nerve-wracking, and many people don't have the time or expertise to do this skillfully. This strategy can also generate additional income taxes on the gains from your investments.

For most people, the most practical way to follow the strategy espoused here is through mutual funds and REITs whose stated goal is investing for income. You can learn more about these at www.morningstar.com and other websites and publications listed in the Resources section at the end of this step. **One warning**: don't chase junk bonds paying the highest interest rates or stocks paying the highest dividends, as these investments have their own special risks.

And even if you need to make withdrawals of principal, I still advocate investing for income, since it reduces the need to sell investments to cover your living expenses. In this case, you need to manage your principal withdrawals so you don't need to sell stocks and other long-term investments when the market is down. This means keeping the next one-to-two years' worth of principal withdrawals in cash investments, such as money market funds, short-term CDs and savings accounts. The way to figure the appropriate amount is to add up all your regular annual income from Social Security, pensions, annuities and investment income for the next one to two years and compare that figure to your expected living expenses for the same period. Any shortfall should be invested in cash investments.

An Asset Allocation Strategy to Consider

You can take the above idea one step further and use an approach to allocating your assets called "age-banding." This is a disciplined approach that helps you decide how much risk you can take and still ride out market downturns.

With this strategy, you calculate the amount of your principal withdrawals for the first 10 years of your retirement, and for these amounts, use very conservative investments such as bonds, CDs or conservatively invested mutual funds. This way, you can feel secure that if the market turns down, you have available the money you need for your living expenses for the near future. You won't need to sell investments during a market downturn.

Next, you calculate the amount of your principal withdrawals for the second decade of your retirement; for these assets, you can allocate more to stocks, say from one-third to two-thirds, since you have at least 10 years to ride out market downturns. For assets that you won't use until the third decade of your retirement, you can invest substantial amounts in stocks, say two-thirds or more, since you will have more than 20 years to ride out market downturns.

This strategy requires periodic attention to make the appropriate shifts from stocks to more conservative investments as you live through the age bands. You may need the help of a financial professional to effectively implement this strategy, including analyzing the amount and type of assets to allocate to each band. You can learn more at www.agebander.com, including more on the underlying theory and software to implement this approach. This software also estimates how your living expenses might change throughout your retirement—more on this in Step 8.

What About Gold?

By the way, I haven't mentioned investing in gold, commodities, options, collectibles, artwork or antiques, and that's for a few reasons. First, they don't pay income, and second, it takes time and skill to invest in them successfully. If you want to make money, you have to figure out when to buy low and when to sell high. This usually takes more time and skill than the average working American has. And these types of investments are far from foolproof; they have experienced substantial ups and downs as well. If you have the available time and skills, then go ahead. But be realistic with yourself; if you don't have the time and skills, then let the professionals do the hard work by investing in the other investment vehicles mentioned here.

Of course, you can have other, good reasons for buying these items. You might enjoy purchasing antiques, artwork and collectibles, for instance. In this case, look at them as consumer items, not as investments. You might also think it's a good idea to bury some gold coins in your backyard in case there's a nuclear holocaust, the U.S. is invaded, or there's a total global meltdown. In this case, consider gold as a protection against extreme events, not as an investment that will generate reliable income during your retirement years.

Wrapping Up

I've devoted a large number of pages to investing, but it's time well spent. The crash of 2008-2009 shook the confidence of millions of responsible, working Americans who had diligently been saving money in their 401(k) plans. I even heard a few people say, "My 401(k) is now a *201*(k)."

Well, most people actually lost 20% to 30% during 2008, not 50%. So your 401(k) became a *301*(k), not a *201*(k). In other words, most of us still had 75 or 80 cents on the dollar—bad news, of course, but at least we weren't at zero. In fact, with the gains in 2009 through 2013, your retirement savings might even be more than before the crash – if you stayed invested!

Do you have friends who had said, "I got wiped out! Why did I save for all those years? I should have spent the money instead!" Well, if they hadn't saved anything, their 401(k) balances would now be zero, and then where would they be?

Yes, we were all hit hard. But the world didn't end, so let's just do the best we can going forward. Here's one way to look at it. Suppose you lost $100,000 from the stock market crash, and you were overwhelmed because you thought there's no way you could make up this loss. What you really lost was the *income* that this $100,000 could generate. Step 5 showed that this income might be 4% or 5% of $100,000, or $4,000 to $5,000 per year. So consider this as the amount of part-time wages that you might need to earn to make up for your investment loss; earning this annual amount buys time for your retirement investments to bounce back. Now you've got a more realistic— and more positive— way to view this challenging situation.

For your retirement years, your goal is to decide on an investment strategy that will produce enough money to supplement your other sources of income and help you survive future downturns. Then, when the storms come again, you don't need to be fearful because you're prepared. You can ride out the turmoil, confident that you'll survive until good times return.

When the stock market is skyrocketing and your friends are bragging that they're rolling in money because they're 100% in stocks, don't feel bad because you've limited your stock investments, and certainly don't jump in when the market is high. You've thought through your investment goals and have good reasons for your asset allocation. Many people remember to "stay the course" when times are bad, but this is also good advice when times are good.

It all comes down to this: Thoughtfully plan your asset allocation and investment strategies, considering what type of investor you are and all of your financial resources. Then you'll be able to invest with confidence and peace of mind.

CHECKLIST OF ACTION STEPS FOR STEP 7: MANAGE YOUR INVESTMENT RISK AND INVEST FOR INCOME

- ❑ Learn about different types of assets—their risks, expected returns and role in your retirement portfolio.
- ❑ Determine what type of investor you are, and which investment products and services are appropriate for your risk tolerance and financial knowledge.
- ❑ If you're approaching your retirement years, investigate how you can best transition to investing for income.

HELPFUL RESOURCES

Books

- *Money for Life: Turn Your IRA and 401(k) Into a Lifetime Retirement Paycheck,* by Steve Vernon
- *Live Long & Prosper: Invest in Your Happiness, Health and Wealth for Retirement and Beyond*, by Steve Vernon
- *The Ultimate Dividend Playbook; Income, Insight and Independence for Today's Investor*, by Josh Peters.
- *Your Money or Your Life,* by Joe Dominguez and Vicki Robin

Websites

- www.agebander.com
- www.fidelity.com
- www.kiplinger.com
- money.cnn.com
- www.moneycentral.msn.com
- www.cbsnews.com/moneywatch/retirement
- www.morningstar.com
- www.smartmoney.com
- www.troweprice.com
- www.vanguard.com

Other publications

- *Retirement Weekly,* an online newsletter available at www.marketwatch.com

STEP 8 Adjust Living Expenses to Match Your Retirement Income

Why should you make sure your living expenses are in line with your income from wages, investments and Social Security? In order to protect against the following risks:

- Running out of money
- Stock market or interest rate fluctuations
- High inflation

In the Introduction to this guidebook, I introduced the ***magic formula*** for managing your finances:

$$I > E$$

While most financial planners focus primarily on the "I" part of the formula, it also pays to focus on the "E" part by making every dollar count.

On average, Americans spend 75% of their budget on housing, transportation, food, health and entertainment—in that order. And there's a lot you can do to control your expenses in each of those five areas. Here are just a few suggestions:

- Pay off your mortgage, or downsize by moving to a less expensive house.
- Downsize your vehicles, use cars longer, own just one car or use public transportation.
- Start eating out less, and minimize the number of prepared (read: expensive) foods, snacks and meat you buy at the store.
- Take care of your health by becoming an informed medical consumer, and make changes to your lifestyle that make you a healthier individual.
- When it comes to entertainment expenses, spend just enough to meet your basic needs and buy only what truly makes you happy.

In addition to these five areas, you can also:

- Wait for bargains and sales.
- Share resources with friends and family. One potential win-win idea is to share housing with friends and relatives, or rent out a room to bring in extra income. Not only will you save or earn money, but you might get important social contacts as well.
- Only buy insurance that's necessary. For example, you may no longer need life insurance if your kids are grown and self-sufficient. If you're not working, you may not need disability insurance.

- Pare down those small daily expenses that drip away at your resources, such as buying fast food for lunch or dinner and going out each morning for expensive coffee. Of course, if you can cut back in other major areas, such as housing and transportation, you can keep those small daily treats that make your life better.

Economists have interesting insights into what they call the "utility theory." According to the theory, if you really need something that's lacking in your life, then buying something to meet your basic needs will most likely make you happier. For instance, if you don't own a car, then buying a basic car might truly make your life better. Once you start going beyond your basic needs, however, then going "upscale" really doesn't add much to your happiness. So after buying a basic car that gets you where you need to go, if you trade up to a fancier car, you don't add much to your happiness.

You can see this phenomenon with the consumer ratings of cars. Inexpensive but well-made cars often have customer satisfaction ratings that are equal to or better than much more expensive cars. But those expensive cars can cost two, three or four times as much as the inexpensive ones.

This leads me to a principle I suggest you apply to all your major purchases. Buy "just enough" to meet your needs and only what truly makes you happy. Don't listen to the commercials that tell you that buying their products will make your life so much happier!

Of course, "just enough" is different for everybody, as the following story illustrates. One day I was giving a workshop at a major retailer and was talking about "just enough." An audience member said, "Steve, there's no such thing as just enough shoes!" Just goes to show that "just enough" is in the eye of the beholder. It's still a great concept that will enable you to get your money's worth from all your purchases.

Some Common Challenges

One challenge for some people is "impulse" buying. They go shopping for a specific item and see something else that grabs their attention. Maybe it's on sale—buy it now! Many financial planners suggest that you hold off on all such purchases. Instead, set your intent to just buy the original item you went shopping for. Then wait a few days, weeks or months, and ask yourself, "Do I still need the item that grabbed my attention?" Better yet, ask yourself, "Is this item worth pushing back my retirement freedom, even just a little bit?" Most of the time the answer is no, and you've saved yourself some money. If the answer is still yes, then maybe you really need it and it's a worthwhile purchase.

Are you a recreational shopper, or do you go shopping to ease stress or unhappiness? Then the above tactic is critical for you. I'd also suggest you investigate alternative forms of recreation or therapy that improve your *rest-of-life*, such as calling a friend, listening to music, spending time with a loved one or going for a walk.

Some people consider relocating during their retirement years, and this has the potential for substantially reducing your housing expenses and improving your life. If you decide to move far away from your current home, however, proceed cautiously. I've seen some people move away from their friends and family and all the things that give them meaning and joy, and then miss them so much that they move back. You might see enticing ads for retirement communities, but a potential downside is that they can isolate you from the rest of the world. It can be very healthy to be in the middle of society and mix with people of all ages and from all walks of life. If you're thinking about moving, do your homework carefully, try before you buy—maybe by renting for awhile before committing to the move—and kick it around with your spouse and extended family and friends.

HOMEWORK ITEM: ***Reflect on your major expenditures for housing, transportation, food, health and entertainment.*** Decide what's "just enough" in each area. Are you currently spending more than "just enough"? Can you cut back in some of these areas and still be happy?

CHECKLIST OF ACTION STEPS FOR STEP 8: ADJUST LIVING EXPENSES TO MATCH YOUR RETIREMENT INCOME

- ❑ Prepare a budget of your living expenses before and after retirement. **Worksheet #5: Estimating Your Retirement Expenses** in Section IV provides a simple way to do this. You can also use one of the many good budgeting and money management software programs out there.
- ❑ Do the "just enough" exercise to find out what's "just enough" for you.
- ❑ If you decide to relocate, start your research and discuss this idea with your spouse, partner and/or extended family.

HELPFUL RESOURCES

Books

- *Your Money or Your Life,* by Joe Dominguez and Vicki Robin
- *Live Long & Prosper: Invest in Your Happiness, Health and Wealth for Retirement and Beyond*, by Steve Vernon
- *The Soul of Money*, by Lynne Twist
- *Independent for Life: Homes and Neighborhoods for an Aging America,* edited by Henry Cisneros, Margaret Dyer-Chamberlain, and Jane Hickie
- *Retirement Places Rated: What You Need to Know to Plan the Retirement You Deserve*, by David Savageau

Websites

- www.wowonline.org is the website for Wider Opportunities for Women (WOW). See the Elder Economic Security Initiative (EESI) on the page titled "Our Programs." This contains state-by-state guidelines, budgets and articles on managing your expenses in retirement.
- www.agebander.com offers retirement planning software that enables you to project your living expenses, recognizing how they might change in your retirement years.

STEP 9 Develop a Robust Social Portfolio

There's been a lot of research done lately on what makes people truly satisfied with life. This research confirms what spiritual leaders, psychologists, counselors and our own grandmothers have been telling us for years. We should enjoy the things we've always wanted to do, connect with a supportive network of family and friends, and give back to family, friends and society.

Doing these things will help protect you from these risks:

- Poor health
- Potentially ruinous bills for long-term care expenses
- Depression and serious illness that may follow death of a spouse
- Loneliness, boredom or lack of purpose

When it comes right down to it, in the long run, the nonfinancial aspects of your life are so much more critical than the financial ones. And there are so many things you can do to be happy in your *rest-of-life*:

- Cultivate relationships with people you enjoy spending time with.
- Take time to pursue your passions, interests and hobbies.
- Apply your skills and experience to your family, friends and work in a way that's consistent with your interests and values.
- Contribute to the greater good of your community, country or the world—something larger than yourself.
- Stay useful, productive and engaged in life!

HOMEWORK ITEM: ***Take a few minutes now to reflect on the best moments in your life and the experiences you would like more of in your retirement years, then write them down.*** And think about this, too: Just how much money did these actually take? My guess is, the things you truly enjoy probably don't cost all that much. When I ask this question in my workshops, typical responses have been "spending time with friends and family," "helping in my community," "learning new things," and "traveling." Only the last item involves a lot of money, although even travel can be inexpensive if you're creative.

Dr. Gene Cohen, author of *The Mature Mind*, has developed an interesting way to think about your social life that he calls your "social portfolio." He encourages you to pursue activities and interests in four areas, as summarized below. You should try activities that involve groups of people as well as activities you can pursue on your own. And you should consider both high mobility/high energy activities as well as those that only require low mobility/low energy. As you get older, you may migrate more to activities that require low mobility/low energy. But you should develop these activities while you're younger so you can naturally make the transition to them as you age. By developing a diversified "social portfolio," you can help protect against potential boredom and lack of meaning and purpose as your life situation evolves over time.

Dr. Gene Cohen's "Social Portfolio"

	Group Efforts and Activities	**Individual Efforts and Activities**
High Mobility/ High Energy	Participating in community groups	Individual hobbies or sports, such as jogging or swimming
Low Mobility/ Low Energy	Hosting book/game club at your home	Reading

Note: The examples shown in each cell are there just to get you started.

CHECKLIST OF ACTION STEPS FOR STEP 9: DEVELOP A ROBUST SOCIAL PORTFOLIO

- ❑ Complete your own Social Portfolio to determine which activities you enjoy or want to try.
- ❑ Take steps to diversify your social life and activities.

HELPFUL RESOURCES

Books

- *The Mature Mind*, by Dr. Gene Cohen
- *Aging Well,* by George Valliant
- *Successful Aging,* by John W. Rowe and Robert L. Kahn
- *A Long, Bright Future: Happiness, Health, and Financial Security in an Age of Increased Longevity*, by Laura Carstensen
- *Authentic Happiness*, by Martin Seligman
- *The Art of Happiness*, and *The Art of Happiness at Work*, by the Dalai Lama and Dr. Howard Cutler
- *If I Live to be 100*, by Neenah Ellis
- *The Soul of Money*, by Lynne Twist
- *A Primer in Positive Psychology*, by Christopher Peterson
- *The Retirement Activities Guide: Things to Do When Golf and Grandkids Aren't Enough*, by Bruce Juell

Service and Volunteer Opportunities

- *www.volunteermatch.org*
- *www.usafreedomcorps.gov*
- *www.charitynavigator.com*
- *www.pointsoflight.org*

STEP 10 Become a Student of Retirement and Develop a Professional Team

By becoming a student of retirement and developing your own professional team, you'll help protect yourself against the following risks:

- Bad advice, fraud or theft
- Running out of money
- Recession/deflation reducing value of retirement savings
- Inflation eroding value of fixed pensions and fixed investments
- Dropping interest rates resulting in reduced income
- Poor health
- Potentially ruinous bills for long-term care expenses

In order to create the type of *rest-of-life* you really want, it's important that you take the time to learn more about the details of executing the first nine steps I've outlined in this guidebook. And continue learning through the years so you keep up-to-date on the latest research, products and services that can make your life better. You don't need to be a full-time student; just keep an eye out for the latest articles, magazines, websites and books.

> *"The people who are doing the best job in retirement are those people who have become students of all things in retirement. These are people who don't necessarily have the most money, but they have taken the time and trouble to plan their future. The biggest problem is that many leave their retirement security to chance; they think that somehow it will all work out. While that might work for a lucky few, I can tell you that the people who truly succeed in retirement have sat down with pen and paper and figured out how much money they need to retire."*
>
> — **Robert Powell,** editor of *Retirement Weekly*

In addition to learning about the details in the previous nine steps, you must also understand:

- What are reasonable rates of return for common investments in order to detect unreasonable claims
- Basic information regarding the various investment and insurance products and services available
- How to obtain and pay for professional advice
- Good sources of information (the "Helpful Resources" lists at the end of each step show my favorites)

To help you as a student of retirement, I distribute a free monthly email newsletter that elaborates on certain topics and provides updates as new research, experience and insights become available. It also serves as a helpful reminder to keep on track—something most of us need! There's a signup form on my website, www.restoflife.com, where you can also access an archive of past issues. In addition, this website is a good source for additional learning; I post updates as we gain new insights on our economic environment, post other articles of interest, provide a list of recommended books and websites, and maintain a library of video highlights from *The Quest DVD* and my workshops. I also write a regular blog column on retirement topics for CBS MoneyWatch.

I believe that many people can learn to manage their retirement finances on their own, if they're diligent about being a student of retirement. Many people, however, will want to build a professional team to help them with these action steps. You might want your team to include a financial advisor, investment expert, tax accountant, insurance agent, health professional or estate attorney. You might also want to consider a nutritionist, trainer or spiritual advisor. You may already know people who fit these descriptions—and be employing them, too. No matter whom you choose, make sure they're both qualified and motivated to have your best interests at heart—you don't want people who are just trying to sell you something.

One of the most important people on your team will most likely be someone you hire regarding your retirement investments. You must pay for investment advice—nothing is free (in fact, "free" financial advice is often very costly). But understand what you're getting yourself into before you pay. Here are three common ways to pay for investment advice:

- **An upfront sales charge or commission which can range from 2% to 6% per transaction.** For a $100,000 investment, for instance, the fee can range from $2,000 to $6,000. This is my least favorite way to pay for advice, since the advisor may be motivated to churn your account to continuously earn commissions, or recommend products that pay the highest commissions.
- **A percentage of assets under management.** A charge of 1% is typical. So for $400,000 in retirement investments, for example, you'd pay about $4,000 per year. And after 10 years, you've paid $40,000. This is better than the first option since your advisor should be unbiased in buying and selling investments. However, the costs can certainly add up over time. In addition, they're not totally unbiased. For example, they may not be too keen on buying an annuity, since the money you spend

on an annuity doesn't count as assets under management. Or they may advise you to take a lump sum from a pension plan, since that can increase their assets under management.

- **A flat fee or hourly rate.** Flat fees can range anywhere from $500 to $2,000, while hourly rates usually range from $150 to $300. This is my favorite method of paying for investment and financial advice. If you decide to go this route, work with a planner who'll give you a program that should work for several years, with periodic checkups in case your situation changes or to make sure your plan is up-to-date.

And remember to check the credentials of anyone you hire to help with your investments. Certified Financial Planners (CFP, www.cfp.net) and Chartered Financial Analysts (CFA, www.cfainstitute.org) have substantial education and experience regarding overall financial planning. You can also check the website of the Financial Planning Association (FPA), www.fpanet.org, which lists people with the CFP designation. Another place to look is the website of the National Association of Personal Financial Advisors (NAPFA), www.napfa.org. NAPFA lists financial advisors who don't take commissions and work only on a fee basis. Also, look for new credentials that specialize in retirement planning, such as Retirement Income Certified Professional (RICP), Certified Retirement Counselor (CRC), and Retirement Management Analyst (RMA).

In addition to CFPs and CFAs, you might also find attorneys, accountants or actuaries who offer retirement planning services. Because their professional training doesn't necessarily translate to retirement planning, if they offer services in areas outside their credentials, check how they got the expertise that's relevant to your situation. For example, most Certified Public Accountants (CPAs) work in business accounting and taxation. However, some have taken additional training as Personal Financial Specialists (PFS), and you can find them by going to the website of the American Institute of Certified Public Accountants (AICPA), www.aicpa.org, and searching for "PFS."

An important distinction to make is professional designations vs. licenses. Professional designations such as CFP, CFA and CPA indicate that the person has gone through a set course of training and expertise and has passed proficiency tests. Don't confuse these with licenses to sell investments or insurance. In these cases, the person knows the legal requirements for selling these products but has not necessarily been formally trained to advise you on whether their products are best for your situation.

No matter whom you're thinking of consulting, I advise you to do your homework and apply your common sense. Having the appropriate credentials and working on a fee-only basis doesn't guarantee that the person is competent or trustworthy. Just as there can be good doctors and poor doctors, good politicians and poor politicians, there can be good advisors and poor advisors. Conversely, there are reputable, trustworthy financial advisors out there who don't belong to the organizations mentioned above or take commissions. However, I believe you'll increase your odds of success by working with trained professionals whose compensation aligns with your financial interests.

Some Final Important Thoughts

Take the time to learn about various products and services, decide what products will work best for your situation, develop your own investment philosophy, and then "go shopping" for the products that best fit you. Don't "be sold" an investment or insurance product by a persuasive "advisor" who might be motivated by a large commission. Take control of your future, rather than let others convince you what to buy.

You should also apply the "go shopping" advice to financial advisors. There can be significant differences in philosophy and approach among advisors you might encounter. For example, some advisors strongly promote stock investments while others shy away from them. Some advisors may be aggressive while others may be cautious. Some advisors focus primarily on investing and accumulating wealth as the basis for financial security, while others focus on insurance as the best way to manage your risks. I advocate that you develop your philosophy towards these issues, and then go shopping for the advisor that best fits your circumstances. Be open to their opinions if they differ from yours—you could learn something important that changes your mind. But in the end, you need to be comfortable with their approach and the recommendations they develop for your circumstances.

CHECKLIST OF ACTION STEPS FOR STEP 10: BECOME A STUDENT OF RETIREMENT, AND DEVELOP YOUR PROFESSIONAL TEAM

- ❑ Identify areas you need to learn more about, and take the steps to acquire this knowledge. This can include subscribing to magazines, visiting online websites or buying the appropriate books.
- ❑ Identify areas for which you need professional help, and then build your team. Learn about how to pay for professional financial advice, and find professionals who are unbiased and motivated to have your best interests at heart.

HELPFUL RESOURCES

- See all the resources listed previously.
- To find trained financial planners, see www.cfp.net, www.fpanet.org, www.napfa.org, www.cfainstitute.org, or the PFS section in www.aicpa.org.
- To find advisors who have taken specialized training in retirement planning, visit www.infre.org/CertifiedRetirementCounselor.shtml, www.theamericancollege.edu/financial-planning/ricp-retirement-income-planning, or http://riia-usa.org/training/rma.asp
- Visit www.nefe.org, the website of the National Endowment for Financial Education.

SECTION III

PUTTING IT ALL TOGETHER

The information I've outlined in the previous section, "**10 Steps to Retirement Security,**" gives you the foundation you need to enjoy health, happiness and financial security in your *rest-of-life*. Now let's put it together so that you can answer the following questions:

- How can I fill the gap between my *Income* ("I") and my *Expenses* ("E")?
- When can I retire?
- How much do I need to save?

How Much Do You Need?

Conventional wisdom says that to have a comfortable retirement, you'll need a retirement income that's equal to 70% to 100% of your pay just before retirement. Retirement planners call this the "replacement ratio" method.

Here's how to figure it out for yourself:

Your annual pay before retirement		**Annual income needed in retirement**
________________	**x .7** =	________________
________________	**x 1.0** =	________________

The above amounts are pre-income tax amounts. This formula defines the range of retirement income that experts say is needed. What's behind this conventional wisdom? There are several reasons you might need less income during retirement than you did while you were working:

- Income taxes go down.
- You'll have no more FICA or other payroll taxes to pay.
- You can reduce or eliminate your work-related expenses, such as commuting or special clothes.
- You're no longer saving for retirement.
- Child-related expenses are reduced or go away completely.
- You might pay off the mortgage on your home or otherwise reduce your monthly expenses.

On the other hand, you might need more income during retirement because:

- Medical expenses go up.
- You're taking care of dependent parents or helping your adult children.
- You're traveling more or are pursuing more hobbies and activities.

The money needed during retirement will be different for everybody, which leads us to a better solution than the "replacement ratio" method. Instead of relying on a figure determined by someone else, define the income you need to support the life you want. In other words, how much do you need to meet your living needs and be happy?

To estimate your own expenses in retirement, you can use **Worksheet #5: Estimating Your Retirement Expenses** in Section IV. Alternatively, there are various software budgeting programs that you could use. If you want to calculate your personal replacement ratio, you can use **Worksheet # 6: Estimating Your Replacement Ratio** in Section IV. That worksheet takes the expenses you estimated in **Worksheet #5** and divides by your current income. You don't need to calculate your own replacement ratio to use the remaining worksheets; it's primarily for your own interest and for you to compare to the conventional wisdom.

Estimating Your Gap

Now let's put your information to work by figuring out your "ballpark estimate." First, turn to **Worksheet #7: Calculating the Gap Between Your Income and Your Needs** in Section IV. Fill in the amount you've determined you'll need for retirement (that's what you figure out on **Worksheet #5: Estimating Your Retirement Expenses**). Then subtract the income you can expect from your employer's pension, Social Security, your current retirement savings and any other source of income you'll have access to. The resulting figure is the gap in income that you'll need to make up from future savings or from work in retirement.

Figuring out the gap helps you determine how much additional savings you'll need to acquire between now and the time you retire. The ballpark estimate converts that additional savings amount to what you'll need to save each year between now and when you retire. In other words, it tells you how much to save to make sure your "I" is greater than your "E."

You can estimate the total additional resources you'd need today to close the gap using **Worksheet #8: Estimating Additional Resources Needed to Close the Gap** in Section IV.

An important part of the process is estimating how much money you'll need to generate a specific amount of lifetime retirement income that increases for inflation. While spreadsheets and calculators give you refined answers, I like to start with simple rules of thumb:

- **A very safe amount**—an amount that's very likely to generate the retirement income you need for the rest of your life— is to take the annual income you need and multiply it by 33. So if you need $20,000 per year to supplement Social Security and other sources of income, you'll need $660,000 in assets to generate this income. This assumes you'll live off just the interest and dividends during your retirement years, and corresponds to Retirement Income Generator (RIG) #1 that I described in Step 5 in Section II.

- **A conservative amount** can be estimated by taking the annual income you need and multiplying it by 25. So if you need $20,000 per year to supplement Social Security and other sources of income, you'll need $500,000 in assets to generate this income. This assumes you'll withdraw 4% per year from your assets and corresponds to RIG #2 that I also described in Step 5. This amount might be needed if you retire in your mid-60s.
- **An aggressive amount** can be settled on if you take the annual income you need and multiply it by 20. So if you need $20,000 per year to supplement Social Security and other sources of income, you'll need $400,000 in assets to generate this income. This assumes you'll withdraw 5% per year from your assets and also corresponds to RIG #2 or a fixed immediate annuity under RIG #3. This amount might be appropriate if you retire in your late 60s or after.

How Much Do You Need to Save?

The next step is to calculate how much you need to save each month to close the gap, using **Worksheet #9: Estimating Monthly Savings Needed to Close the Gap** in Section IV. Next to using a spreadsheet or an online calculator, this is the best way to determine how much to save.

But maybe you want it boiled down even further. If that's the case, then you have a few choices when it comes to saving for your retirement. These options all assume you're still working. Here they are:

- Increase your current savings by 1% of your pay. This small amount won't put much of a dent in your disposable income and will help you achieve your retirement goals. Then increase it again by 1% of your pay every six months, until you're saving what you need.
- Set aside the maximum matched by your employer in your savings plan at work. If you aren't saving this amount, you're leaving money on the table.
- Start saving 10% to 15% of your pay. Put aside these amounts for 25 to 30 years, and you'll most likely be in the ballpark when you're ready to retire, provided you follow the other steps in this guidebook.

Using Online Calculators and Tutorials

This book contains simple methods and worksheets for estimating how much money you'll need to retire and how much to save. Most likely, the results will help you get close to estimating the resources you need; you can then make adjustments as life unfolds. For some people, that might be good enough.

Others may want to work with a qualified professional advisor to estimate their retirement needs. If you decide to take this route, I recommend you not turn off your brain and assume everything will turn out OK now that you have someone looking out for you. It still pays to understand the tools and methods your advisor uses and have informed discussions regarding your specific strategies.

For those of you with the time and inclination, I recommend using an online retirement planning calculator or spreadsheets to refine your analyses. These calculators can go into much more detail than simple worksheets and rules of thumb. In some cases, these calculators are accompanied by tutorials that can be a good source of information and insights.

Using the calculators will take some time and effort, and you should prepare yourself for some frustration. I've looked at many calculators and have often been confused at first; I had to poke around for awhile or call the help desk before I finally understood how to answer the questions or interpret the results. I know this sounds like a lot of work, but it sure beats being wrong and going broke at age 80! And it's really not that much time, given the importance.

As you can imagine, there are all kinds of retirement planning calculators out there. Some are available to the general public and can be found on the websites of nonprofit financial education institutions, online financial magazines or some financial institutions. Some are available only if you are invested with a particular financial institution or are accessible through your employer or 401(k) plan. And some you must purchase. The Resources section at the end of this chapter has a list of calculators that I'm familiar with, but it isn't intended to be an exhaustive list.

Most calculators use a process that's similar to the simplified worksheets in this book. They estimate your retirement income from all sources, compare the results to your projected expenses, estimate a shortfall between your income and expenses, and figure out how much you need to save to make up for the shortfall. They also help you decide when you can retire, how much you can withdraw each year from your retirement savings, and how you might allocate your assets among different types of investments.

These calculators vary in the level of detail they ask you to input and in the resulting output. Some are simple and easy to understand, while others require substantial effort to use and interpret. Some use sophisticated techniques called "Monte Carlo" or "stochastic" projections. These run 1,000 or more simulations of the future under a variety of possible future economic scenarios regarding rates of return and inflation, and they calculate the chances of various outcomes. For example, the output might say something like this:

- **Optimistic results:** There's a 5% chance your total annual retirement income will be $75,000 *or more.*
- **Average or median results:** There's a 50% chance your total annual retirement income will be $55,000 *or more.*
- **Pessimistic results:** There's a 5% chance your total annual retirement income will be $40,000 *or less.*

Other calculators use much more simple projections, such as assuming fixed rates for your asset return and inflation. In this case, the results show that either you meet your goals or you don't, *based on those assumptions.*

To help you make the best use of these calculators, I'd like to suggest you adhere to the following guidelines. First, don't make the common mistake of assuming that the projections must be right because they were produced by a sophisticated computer program. All calculators prepare estimations of future results based on making various assumptions. Often these assumptions are based on historical data. These assumptions can easily turn out to be wrong if the future turns out differently from the historical data. No model can take all possibilities into account. Even the most sophisticated computer models use simplifying assumptions which may overlook possibilities that later might actually happen.

As a result, I recommend you run the projections several times, each time varying such assumptions as assumed investment returns, assumed withdrawal rates from your retirement savings, your asset allocation, how long you expect to live, and your retirement age. Remember—a main goal of this book is to help you survive future downturns. This means you should project what will happen to your financial situation assuming that such events will occur in the future, and put strategies in place to protect you in case these events happen.

If you use a Monte Carlo or stochastic system, focus on the results for the pessimistic scenarios, for the following reason. Suppose you withdraw from your retirement savings the amounts associated with the median or average forecast. According to the computer program, you have a 50/50 chance of outliving your retirement savings! Not good odds for such an unpleasant outcome. I'd prefer you have much lower odds of outliving your savings—say, one out of 10. In this case, you'd need to withdraw according to a forecast that had a 90% success rate—often called a 90% confidence level.

I also suggest you use two or three different calculators and compare the results. If they produce different answers, it's probably not the case that one is wrong and one is right. Each will use its own methodology and assumptions. Understand how each works so you can understand the reasons for the differences in output. Eventually you might settle on a favorite calculator, which is OK after you've initially made the effort to investigate a few others.

Many calculators ask you how long you expect to live. To answer this question, it's a good idea to use one of the life expectancy calculators described in the Introduction—then add five to 10 years to make sure you'll have enough resources in case you live longer than expected.

I favor online calculators over simple worksheets and guessing (which, according to one survey, is by far the most common method of determining how much money you need to retire). Here are some features I prefer:

- The ability to input your expected expenses in retirement for various types of expenditures, instead of using simple replacement ratios or a fixed total target income. I'd rather that you get prompted to remember all the things you might spend money on, taking into account your specific spending needs.

- The ability to vary how much you'll withdraw from your savings, so you can see the effect of reducing or increasing your withdrawals.
- Storing your answers and results. Not only will this save you a lot of time when you revisit the calculator, but it helps you compare current and prior projections.
- The ability to vary the future economic scenarios, either with Monte Carlo analyses or by inputting different economic assumptions. You'll want to see what might happen if we get hit again with a downturn.
- Output that shows the component income sources—Social Security, draw from retirement savings, pension if applicable, and work. It's important to understand how the different pieces add up to your total income.
- "What if" features. For example, what if you work for a specified period in your retirement years, what if you sell your house and invest the proceeds, what if you reduce your living expenses, what if you delay retirement, what if you live longer than expected, what if you have high long-term care expenses, what if you change your allocation between different types of investments, what if you delay taking Social Security benefits, and so on.

While I haven't completed an exhaustive review of available online calculators, I have found that the Retirement Income Planner on the website of Fidelity Investments has many of the above features, and it's available to anybody. One of the most detailed online planners I've seen, available for purchase at www.RetirementWorks2.com, is called RW2 for YOU. In particular, I like that it projects your results using alternative future scenarios, helping you understand how to withstand the risks of different possible economic and life events.

When entering your expected living expenses, don't overlook large, future "one time" expenses such as replacing your car, replacing the roof on your house, etc. If you'll be retired for 20 or more years, such replacement items are inevitable. Also, factor in that you might have high expenses for long-term care in your later years. Finally, you may want to consider that you might spend money on dependent parents, if that applies to you.

Of course, you need to remember to update your projections periodically to take into account changes in your situation, such as account values that have changed due to stock market fluctuations, changes in spending or saving habits, and so on.

Warning: Some calculators choose for you the method of converting retirement savings to annual retirement income. These might be OK if you're more than 10 years away from retirement and you just want to see if you're on track. But once you get closer to retirement, you should be thinking about the method you'll use to withdraw from your retirement savings, and project your situation using that method. As you saw in Step 5, there are various methods for withdrawing from your retirement savings with widely varying results. If you use a calculator that chooses this method for you, you may not get answers that best fit your situation.

Finally, apply a good dose of common sense when interpreting the results. One calculator told me to invest a significant part of my retirement savings in state and municipal bonds. As I write this, headlines are screaming that some state and local governments are busting their budgets and there's a chance of bankruptcy, however small. The computer model was based on historical returns and default rates, which have been virtually nonexistent. However, it didn't and can't predict scenarios that haven't happened before but nevertheless could happen in the future, such as the failings of politics and governments.

Two very important decisions you need to make involve how to allocate your assets among different types of investments and how much to withdraw each year from your retirement savings. Online calculators can give you valuable insights about these decisions. However, I strongly advocate that you don't make these decisions based exclusively on the median or average scenario produced by a computer forecast, for the reasons stated previously. I'd rather have sources of retirement income and investments that protect me *in case* we have high inflation or another meltdown, even if a computer model tells me that these events are unlikely to happen. I'll cover this subject more in the next few pages.

I'd also keep in mind the following when making decisions based on computer projections: The future disappointment and damage to your life that will occur if you fall far short of forecasts is much greater than the potential excitement and gains of exceeding these forecasts. This means adopting strategies that have a very high chance of producing an income stream that covers your living expenses for the rest of your life, no matter what happens in the economy and no matter how long you live. Have peace of mind by planning for the worst, and then enjoy life if the worst doesn't happen.

You've Come Up Short. Now What?

Many people who do the ***I* > *E*** analysis come up short by substantial amounts. What now, they think? The only possibilities are some combination of:

- Postponing retirement
- Working part time or full time during your retirement years to supplement your financial resources
- Reducing spending before retirement so you can save more for retirement
- Reducing spending during retirement
- Tinkering with withdrawal strategies for your retirement savings or your target amounts of savings needed

Then you can recalculate the ***I* > *E*** analysis to see where you stand. It may take you several times before you come up with a plan that works for you, but keep at it. You'll succeed if you persist.

There are several strategies you can implement for increasing your total "I" or decreasing your total "E," and they are described in Steps 1 through 10 in Section II. You may want to go back and revisit these steps to see how you can make changes that will help balance your "I" and "E."

Diversify Your Retirement Income

As we discussed in Step 5 of Section II, an important refinement of investment diversification is income diversification. Because you never know what the future can hold, you want to have different sources of retirement income that can withstand various types of economic challenges. This will help protect your retirement income no matter what comes along. Table 11 summarizes why this is an important goal.

Table 11. How Various Retirement Income Sources Fare in Different Economic Climates

Income Source	"Normal" Times[1]	Recession/Deflation	High Inflation
Social Security	Good	Best	Good
Pension/Annuity	Good	Best	Poor
Stocks	Best	Poor	Mixed
Bonds	Good	Best	Poor
Cash[2]	Poor	Good	Mixed
Real estate	Good	Poor	Mixed
Hard Assets[3]	Poor	Poor	Best
Wages	Good	Good/Poor	Good

[1] *Low inflation, steady economic growth*
[2] *T-bills, money market funds, FDIC-insured savings accounts*
[3] *Gold, silver, commodities, collectibles*

I realize this is a complicated chart, and there's no need to memorize it. Let me just make some general observations:

- Note that the only sources of income that do well in all three economic scenarios are Social Security benefits and wages. This is one reason why maximizing your Social Security income and keeping your feet in the job market are good strategies.
- The "good/poor" rating for wages in a recession reflects the fact that it can be challenging to find paid work during a recession. If you find a job, wages rate as "good." But it's a risk to rely heavily on wage income if you're employed in a job that's vulnerable to layoffs and that's reflected in the "poor" rating.
- Every other source of income does well in some climates and poorly in others. Since it's very hard to predict when these economic climates will occur, a sound strategy is to diversity your sources of income so you're not vulnerable to a particular type of economic downturn.
- With stocks, bonds and cash, the ratings work whether you're living on just the income (RIG#1 from Step 5) in Section II or are withdrawing principal (RIG #2 from Step 5). However, if you're just living on the income, you're less vulnerable to economic downturns compared to withdrawing principal.

Another way of thinking about this is to assess the quality of your retirement income from each source. When you look at projections from an online calculator, $1,000 of monthly income from Social Security looks the same as a $1,000 withdrawal from your 401(k) plan, but there are significant differences in the quality of these incomes. Below is a checklist for the quality of retirement income; the more boxes you can check with a "yes" answer, the higher the reliability and ability to withstand various economic challenges.

Table 12. Checklist for the Quality of Retirement Income

- ☐ Is the income guaranteed by a reliable institution to be paid for the rest of your life?
- ☐ Will the income continue to your spouse or other dependents after you die?
- ☐ Does your income remain unchanged if there's a market downturn?
- ☐ Does your income increase for inflation?
- ☐ Does your income have special tax advantages?

The best conclusion you can draw from Tables 11 and 12 is to increase the quality of your retirement income and to have different sources of income; these strategies decrease your vulnerability to various types of economic downturns and challenges.

Next Steps

So now what? At the beginning of this guidebook, I said there was a lot more you needed to do than simply read this guidebook. Here are a few more things you can do in the next year or two that will help you create the best *rest-of-life* possible:

- Involve your spouse or partner, or form or join a small group of friends to plan together. Research suggests that the best way to make positive changes in your life is to have the support of people who care about you.
- Develop a realistic life plan that includes your best answers for the **"Top 10 Retirement Decisions"** listed at the beginning of this guidebook.
- Make contingency plans for life events. You've got to figure out:
    - What would happen if you or your spouse dies?
    - Are your beneficiary designations accurate?
    - Do you have a will?
    - What will you do if you're no longer able to care for yourself or your spouse?

Over the next several years, you should also discuss and consider:

- Working in your later years. Where will you do it and for how long?
- Living situation. Where do you want to live? Will you need to downsize? Or move to a different area?

- Hobbies and activities. What will you do with your time?

Then make a list of action steps and prioritize them. What will you do tomorrow? Next week? Next month? Next year? You don't need to do everything all at once, but you do need to make steady progress over the next few years if you want to accomplish your goals.

Final Thoughts

It should be obvious by now that I strongly advocate planning ahead in order to achieve success in your retirement years. But we also need to realize the limitations of planning—specifically that life can turn out much different from what you planned, in spite of your best intentions. Unforeseen future events such as stock market crashes, natural disasters, accidents or just plain bad luck can mess up the best of plans. But that's not a good reason to give up on planning. Instead, plan for what's most likely to happen, given the best insights and information available to you, with contingency plans in case the unlikely occurs.

You'll increase your chances of surviving unfavorable events if you have good health, enough money in a safe place, skills and contacts that are useful to society, and a network of family and friends who care about you and will band together in case of an emergency. And who knows—maybe the unforeseen event will be good luck or good fortune, in which case your resources will give you the best chance of reaping the most from your good luck!

Our society in general—and advertising in particular—both send us powerful messages that full-time retirement is the right way to complete your life, that you're a failure if you can't retire, or that you've been cheated out of life if you can't retire. I think that's just not true. I've presented alternative ways of thinking about your later years that I believe are more realistic and practical for most Americans, options that may be healthier and more enjoyable compared to the traditional full-time retirement.

I suggest you consider alternative goals for your later years: long life, health and prosperity. Then determine the steps you need to take and measure your progress against these new goals. Your life will be better for it!

Everyone needs a basic guide for important life decisions, and the steps in this guidebook are a good place to start. And while the strategies I've included should work for most people, other strategies might work as well. Find out what works for you! This is your life and your future: Put in place solid plans, so you can focus on enjoying your *rest-of-life*. Have confidence that you can live until age 90—or even 100—and still enjoy life.

Good luck!

CHECKLIST OF ACTION STEPS FOR PUTTING IT ALL TOGETHER

- ❑ Complete your needs and gap analyses to determine when you can retire and how much you need to save. Decide whether you'll use spreadsheets or online calculators or the simple worksheets in this guidebook.
- ❑ Examine your various sources of retirement income to make sure they are diversified and of the highest possible quality.
- ❑ Repeat the calculations until you get a plan that makes sense for you.

HELPFUL RESOURCES

Websites

- Visit www.restoflife.com for extra copies of the worksheets in Section IV.
- Online financial magazines and websites: www.cbsnews.com/moneywatch/retirement, www.smartmoney.com, www.kiplinger.com, money.cnn.com
- Financial institutions: www.fidelity.com, www.schwab.com, www.troweprice.com, www.vanguard.com. In particular, Fidelity's website has a comprehensive retirement income planner, and T. Rowe Price's website has a good calculator to help you determine how much to withdraw from 401(k) accounts.
- www.moneyforlifeguideonline.com is a compendium of helpful blog posts and articles.
- www.morningstar.com, which rates mutual funds and has retirement planning calculators.
- www.ssa.gov, the official website for the Social Security Administration
- www.choosetosave.org, the website of the American Savings Council which includes a simple online retirement calculator
- www.nefe.org, the website of the National Endowment for Financial Education
- www.RetirementWorks2.com, which offers a very detailed planner available for purchase. It includes projections under alternative future scenarios, which helps you understand how to withstand the risks of different possible economic and life events that are detrimental.
- www.agebander.com, which offers retirement planning software that projects your total retirement income and enables you to compare this to estimates of your living expenses, which have been projected recognizing how they might change during your retirement years.

SECTION IV

APPENDIX AND WORKSHEETS

These simple worksheets are intended to help you build sufficient financial resources during your retirement years. They use simple approximations that get you in the ballpark of developing the financial resources you need to support the life you want. For more refined analyses, use computer programs, spreadsheets or any of the online calculators that are listed in the Resources sections throughout this guidebook. Visit www.restoflife.com for additional copies of the worksheets in this section.

These worksheets express the results in terms of today's dollars to make it easier for you to understand the results and compare them to your current income and savings levels. The key results take into account future inflation when estimating the amount of assets you need and how much you need to save (both in terms of today's dollars).

Appendix A: Hopes and Dreams vs. Fears and Concerns

Worksheets

1. Retirement Resources Inventory
2. Estimating Your Total Retirement Income
3. Estimating Income From Savings/401(k) Plans
4. Factors for Projecting Savings Balances
5. Estimating Your Retirement Expenses
6. Estimating Your Replacement Ratio
7. Calculating the Gap Between Your Income and Your Needs
8. Estimating Additional Total Savings Needed to Close the Gap
9. Estimated Monthly Savings Needed to Close the Gap
10. Savings Accumulation Factors

Appendix A

Hopes and Dreams

Fears and Concerns

Worksheet #1

Retirement Resources Inventory

Defined benefit pension plans

Current plan
Plan name: ______________________
Normal retirement age (NRA): __________

Estimated monthly
retirement income

- At NRA: __________
- Reduced for
  spouse's coverage: __________
- At early retirement: __________
- Reduced for
  spouse's coverage: __________

Vested benefit from prior employer, if any
Plan name: ______________________
Normal retirement age (NRA): __________

Estimated monthly
retirement income

- At NRA: __________
- Reduced for
  spouse's coverage: __________
- At early retirement: __________
- Reduced for
  spouse's coverage: __________

401(k) plans/IRAs/Savings

401(k)/403(b)/457 saving plans

Current plan balance: __________
as of __________

Other plan balance: __________
as of __________

Other plan balance: __________
as of __________

IRAs

First IRA balance: __________
as of __________

Second IRA balance: __________
as of __________

Savings/Investment Institutions

First balance: __________
as of __________

Second balance: __________
as of __________

Grand total: __________

Notes to the Retirement Resources Inventory Worksheet

- Include spouse's benefits, if applicable
- Use extra pages, if necessary. Go to www.restoflife.com to print more.
- For savings, do not include the value of assets that you don't intend to use to generate retirement income. For example, don't include the value of homes, cars, jewelry, etc. *unless* you plan to sell them and use the proceeds to generate retirement income. If this is the case, reduce any sales proceeds by applicable taxes and selling costs.

WORKSHEET # 2

Estimating Your Total Retirement Income

PREPARED ON: ____________

YOUR CURRENT AGE: ____________

1. Desired retirement age		
2. Years until retirement age		
3. Estimated Social Security monthly income at retirement age (include spousal benefits)		
4. Estimated total monthly defined benefit pension*: Plan 1 ________ Plan 2 ________ Plan 3 ________		
5. Total monthly draw from savings/401(k) balances (see Worksheet #3)		
6. Other income		
7. Total monthly income (3) + (4) + (5) + (6)		

**Apply appropriate reductions for joint and survivor election and early retirement, if applicable.*

WORKSHEET #3

Estimating Income From Savings/401(k) Plans

Desired retirement age		
1. Total savings/401(k) balances (from Retirement Resources Inventory, Worksheet #1)		
2. Enter factor appropriate for years until retirement (see Worksheet #4)		
3. Projected account balance at desired retirement age: (1) times (2)		
4. Projected annual income Simplified approaches: ▪ Multiply (3) by .03 if use income method ▪ Multiply (3) by .04 or .05 for withdrawing income plus principal* ▪ If you want to buy an annuity, input item (3) into calculator at www.immediateannuities.com		
5. Total monthly income (4) divided by 12		

**Use .04 for retirement in your mid 60s.*
Use .05 for retirement in your late 60s or after. Use an online calculator for a more refined approach.

Note: Suppose you decide to use two methods of withdrawing from your savings, as described in Step 5. In this case, complete this form twice—once for each withdrawal method and the amount you apply to each method. Then add the results together to determine your total retirement income.

WORKSHEET #4

Factors for Projecting Savings Balances

YEARS UNTIL RETIREMENT	FACTOR
1	1.03
2	1.06
3	1.09
4	1.13
5	1.16
6	1.19
7	1.23
8	1.27
9	1.30
10	1.34
11	1.38
12	1.43
13	1.47
14	1.51
15	1.56
16	1.60
17	1.65
18	1.70
19	1.75
20	1.81
25	2.09
30	2.43

Assumes 3% real growth. In other words, it adjusts for future inflation. Interpolate the factor for partial years.

WORKSHEET #5

Estimating Your Retirement Expenses

Regular Expenses	Current *Monthly* Expenses	Estimated *Monthly* Retirement Expenses
Mortgage or rent	________	________
Utilities, telephone	________	________
Groceries	________	________
Work expenses (commuting, lunches, etc.)	________	________
Entertainment, eating out	________	________
Recreation (boating, hobbies, etc.)	________	________
Clothing	________	________
Laundry, cleaning	________	________
Personal (hair cuts, health club)	________	________
Auto operation	________	________
Other transportation	________	________
Education (adult courses)	________	________
Education of children (college expenses, etc.)	________	________
Donations	________	________
Support of others (alimony, elderly relative)	________	________
Loans (auto, other)	________	________
Regular services (lawn service, etc.)	________	________
Other: ________________	________	________
Total Regular Expenses	*$* ________	*$*________

Periodic Expenses	Current Expenses *(Annual)*	Estimated Retirement Expenses *(Annual)*
Property taxes	________	________
Household maintenance and repair	________	________
New major household purchases and repairs (appliances, new roof, etc.)	________	________
Casualty insurance premiums (auto, home, etc.)	________	________
Life, disability, medical insurance premiums	________	________
Vacations	________	________
Gifts (birthdays, anniversaries, holidays)	________	________
Income taxes (local, state, federal)	________	________
Legal services	________	________
Medical, dental, veterinarian	________	________
Savings/investment deposits	________	________
Miscellaneous expenses	________	________
Other: ________________	________	________
Total Periodic Expenses	*$* ________	*$* ________

* *Assume prices will be the same as they are today.*

Total Regular Expenses:	**$**__________	**$**__________
times 12 = Total Annual:	$__________	**$** _________
plus		
Total Periodic Expenses:	**$**__________	**$**__________
equals		
Total Annual Expenses:	**$**__________	**$**__________
	Estimated Annual Current Expenses	**Estimated Annual Retirement Expenses**

WORKSHEET #6

Estimating Your Replacement Ratio

1. Total annual retirement expenses from Worksheet #5 (from the box at the bottom, the number at the bottom of the last column)	
2. Your current annual income before income taxes and FICA taxes are taken out	
3. Your replacement ratio (item 1 divided by item 2)	

WORKSHEET #7

Calculating the Gap Between Your Income and Your Needs

	Retire at age ____	Retire at age ____
1. Annual income needed (total annual retirement expenses from Worksheet #5)		
2. Minus annual Social Security		
3. Minus annual pension income		
4. Minus annual draw from savings		
5. Equals the gap in annual income, to be closed by future savings or work		

WORKSHEET #8

Estimating Additional Total Savings Needed to Close the Gap

	Retire at age ___	Retire at age ___
1. Gap in income needed (from item #5 on Worksheet #7)		
2. Factor Use 33 (safest) Use 25 (conservative) Use 20 (most aggressive)		
3. Total additional savings needed at retirement: (1) times (2)		

WORKSHEET #9

Estimating Monthly Savings Needed to Close the Gap

	Retire at age ____	Retire at age ____
1. Additional savings needed (from item #3 on Worksheet #8)		
2. Years until retirement		
3. Factor appropriate for years until retirement (see the Savings Accumulation Factor on Worksheet #10)		
4. Needed monthly savings: (1) times (3)		

WORKSHEET #10

Savings Accumulation Factors

YEARS UNTIL RETIREMENT	FACTOR
1	.0820
2	.0404
3	.0265
4	.0196
5	.0154
6	.0127
7	.0107
8	.0092
9	.0081
10	.0071
11	.0064
12	.0058
13	.0052
14	.0048
15	.0044
16	.0041
17	.0038
18	.0035
19	.0033
20	.0030
25	.0022
30	.0017

Assumes 3% real growth. In other words, it adjusts for future inflation. It also assumes monthly contributions. Interpolate the factor for partial years.

ABOUT THE AUTHOR

Steve Vernon worked as a consulting actuary for more than 35 years, helping large employers design and manage their retirement programs. During that time, he worked on the front lines of the tremendous shift in retirement plans that took place over the past three decades. Until the 1980s, most employers took care of you in retirement with traditional pension and retiree medical plans. Now most people only have 401(k) plans and no retiree medical coverage from their employer. This places a tremendous responsibility on individuals to generate an income that lasts for life and to protect against the threat of large expenses for medical and long-term care.

Several surveys show that baby boomers are struggling with these issues and that they need help. Steve's training and experience as an actuary puts him in a unique position to provide guidance. In 2006, he retired from his position as a vice president and consulting actuary at a large human resources consulting firm. He then founded *Rest-of-Life* Communications, which is dedicated to providing trusted, realistic and unbiased information and strategies to help working people plan for their retirement years.

Actuaries are professionals who measure the risks of important but unpredictable life events—risks such as death, serious illness, accidents and outliving your money during retirement. Living too long is considered a risk! To mitigate these risks, actuaries design financial programs such as life insurance, medical insurance, pension plans and 401(k) plans. Steve is a Fellow in the Society of Actuaries, and currently serves on their Committee for Post-Retirement Needs and Risks. He is also a Consulting Research Scholar at the Stanford Center on Longevity, where he assists with research on retirement income strategies and behavioral finance. In addition, he writes a regular blog column on retirement topics for CBS MoneyWatch.

Steve and *Rest-of-Life* Communications has served a diverse group of clients such as AARP, Aerospace Corporation, Chicago Transit Authority, Esterline Corporation, Huntington Hospital, the International Foundation of Employee Benefit Plans, Merrill Lynch, the National Press Foundation, Portland General Electric, Puget Sound Energy, Raytheon Company, the Royal Bank of Canada, Sempra Energy, Times Mirror Corp., United Centers for Spiritual Living, USC and Weyerhaeuser Corporation.

Steve lives in Oxnard, California with his wife, Melinda, where they're following the advice in this book for their *rest-of-life*. For more information, visit www.restoflife.com or email Steve at steve.vernon@restoflife.com.

VOCAB

for the College Bound

LEVEL

10

2nd Edition

Revised and Expanded

ISBN 978-1-620191-125

Senior Editor: Paul Moliken

Editor: Darlene Gilmore

Cover & Text Design: Larry Knox

Layout: Chris Koniencki

P.O. Box 658 Clayton, Delaware 19938 ō www.prestwickhouse.com

Item No. 309269

Table *of* Contents

Strategies for Completing Activities

Strategies *for* Completing Activities

Words in Context

One way you can make sure that you understand what an unfamiliar word means is to see it used in a sentence and make a guess, an inference, as to its meaning. For example, you probably do not know what the word *theriomorphic* means. Using roots, prefixes, and suffixes will help, as you will see explained below. Read it in the following sentence, though, and you will have another method to arrive at its meaning:

> The drawing on the clay tablet that archaeologists recently discovered depicted a man with antlers and hooves—a *theriomorphic* being—within a ring of fire.

Clues in the sentence enable you to see the context of *theriomorphic*: a primitive drawing showing something not completely human. Therefore, you can infer that *theriomorphic* means "a person who looks like an animal."

Here's another example:

> Dawn was a *somnambulist*; on some nights, her family found her in the hall, other times she was discovered in the basement, and once, they found her sitting asleep in the front seat of the car.

After reading the sentence, you should be able to infer that the word *somnambulist* must mean "someone who walks in his or her sleep."

Roots, Prefixes, and Suffixes

To the person interested in words, a knowledge of roots, prefixes, and suffixes turns each new, unfamiliar word into a puzzle. And while it is a sure and lifelong way to build your vocabulary, there are two points to keep in mind.

1. Some words have evolved through usage so that today's definitions are different from the ones you might have inferred from an examination of their roots and/or prefixes. For example, the word *abstruse* contains the prefix *ab–* (away) and the root *trudere* (to thrust) and literally means "to thrust away." But today, the word is used to describe something that is "hard to understand."

2. Occasionally, you may be incorrect about a root. For example, knowing that the root *vin* means "to conquer," you would be correct in concluding that the word *invincible* means "not able to be conquered"; but if you tried to apply that root meaning to the word *vindictive* or *vindicate*, you would miss the actual meaning. So, in analyzing an unfamiliar word, check for other possible roots than the one you first assumed if your inferred meaning doesn't fit the context.

These warnings notwithstanding, a knowledge of roots, prefixes, and suffixes is one of the best ways to build a strong, vital vocabulary.

Usage Inferences

The next method of determining if you understand what a word means is for you to see the word as it might be applied to various situations. Therefore, in a Usage Inference, you need to be able to take the definition you learned into the real world. Remembering the definition and using the word correctly are two different concepts. We supply a series of multiple-choice situations in which you need to figure out the best use of the word.

Let's assume that you learned in a lesson that *specious* means "false or faulty reasoning that seems true" or "an argument that does not stand up to logical reasoning."

Example:

When or where would making a *specious* argument most likely be challenged?
A. on Friday night asking for the keys to the family car
B. in a jury room debating the guilt of someone on trial
C. with your family deciding on the price of a trip to Hawaii
D. at school trying to convince your friend to go sky diving

While all the answers could be examples of making a specious argument, the one that might cause a problem is B, simply because any faulty argument would most likely be argued against by another juror. Obviously, faulty logic and arguments can be used in A, B, C, and D. After all, saying the wrong thing may prevent getting the keys, spending too much could ruin a trip, and sky diving is dangerous. These three situations, though, are less likely to have flawed logic called into question.

Another key to the correct answer is stated in the question, so make sure that you read that part carefully, as it frequently will narrow down your choices.

Reading Comprehension

Reading questions generally fall into several types.

1. *Identifying the main idea or the author's purpose. In short, the question asks, "What is this selection about?"*

   In some paragraphs, this is easy to spot because there are one or two ideas that leap from the paragraph. In some selections, however, this may be much more difficult, especially if there are convoluted sentences with clauses embedded within clauses. It also may be difficult in those selections in which there are inverted sentences (a sentence with the subject at the end) or elliptical sentences (a sentence in which a word or words are left out). All of these obstacles can be overcome if you take one sentence at a time and put it in your own words.

Consider the following sentence:

> These writers either jot down their thoughts bit by bit, in short, ambiguous, and paradoxical sentences, which apparently mean much more than they say—of this kind of writing Schelling's treatises on natural philosophy are a splendid instance; or else they hold forth with a deluge of words and the most intolerable diffusiveness, as though no end of fuss were necessary to make the reader understand the deep meaning of their sentences, whereas it is some quite simple if not actually trivial idea, examples of which may be found in plenty in the popular works of Fichte, and the philosophical manuals of a hundred other miserable dunces.

But if we edit out some of the words, the main point of this sentence is obvious.

> These writers either jot down their thoughts bit by bit, in short, ambiguous, and paradoxical sentences, which apparently mean much more than they say—of this kind of writing Schelling's treatises on natural philosophy are a splendid instance; or else they hold forth with a deluge of words and the most intolerable diffusiveness, as though [it] end of fuss were necessary to make the reader understand the deep meaning of their sentences, whereas it is son [a]uite simple if not actually trivial idea, examples of which may be found in plenty in the popular works of Fichte, and the philosophical manuals of a hundred other miserable dunces.

While the previous sentence needs only deletions to make it clear, this next one requires major revisions and must be read carefully and put into the reader's own words.

> Some in their discourse desire rather commendation of wit, in being able to hold all arguments, than of judgment, in discerning what is true; as if it were a praise to know what might be said, and not what should be thought.

After studying it, a reader might revise the sentence as follows:

> In their conversations, some people would rather win praise for their wit or style of saying something rather than win praise for their ability to judge between what is true or false—as if it were better to sound good regardless of the quality of thought.

2. *Identifying the stated or inferred meaning. Simply, what is the author stating or suggesting?*

3. *Identifying the tone or mood of the selection or the author's feeling.*

   To answer this type of question, look closely at individual words and their connotations. For example, if an author describes one person as stubborn and another as firm, it tells you something of the author's feelings. In the same manner, if the author uses many words with harsh, negative connotations, he is conveying one mood; but if he uses words with milder negative connotations, he may be striving for quite another mood.

Pronunciation Guide

ă	pat	ō	boat, oh
ā	aid, fey, pay	o͝o	took
â	air, care, wear, ant	o͞o	boot, fruit
ä	father	ô	ball, haul
b	bib	p	pop
ch	church	r	roar
d	deed	s	miss, sauce, see
ĕ	pet, pleasure	sh	dish, ship
ē	be, bee, easy, leisure	t	tight
f	fast, fife, off, phase, rough	th	path, thin
g	gag	th (underlined)	this, bathe
h	hat	ŭ	cut, rough
hw	which	û	circle, firm, heard, term, turn, urge, word
ĭ	pit	v	cave, valve, vine
ī	by, guy, pie	w	with
î	dear, deer, fierce, mere	y	yes
j	jury, joke	yo͞o	abuse, use
k	kiss, clean, quit	z	rose, size, xylophone, zebra
oi	soil, toy	zh	garage, pleasure, vision
ou	cow, out	ə	about, silent, pencil, lemon, circus
ŏ	closet, bother	ər	butter

LEVEL 10 VOCABULARY for the College Bound

Lesson One

1. **abate** (ə bāt′) *verb* to lessen in violence or intensity
When the winds *abated*, the helicopter was able to land.
syn: subside, decrease *ant*: intensify, increase

2. **abet** (ə bĕt′) *verb* to assist or encourage, especially in wrongdoing
For hiding the thief in his basement, he was charged with aiding and *abetting* a criminal.
syn: promote, incite *ant*: impede, dissuade, deter

3. **abhor** (ăb hôr′) *verb* to detest, loathe, hate strongly
Leigh Ann loved her job, but she *abhorred* the long commute to work every day.
syn: despise, abominate *ant*: love, esteem

4. **acquit** (ə kwĭt′) *verb* to find not guilty of a fault or crime
The jury *acquitted* the man, and he was free to go.
syn: vindicate, absolve, exonerate *ant*: convict, incriminate, condemn

5. **acrimony** (ă′ krə mō nē) *noun* harsh temper or bitter feeling
Because of his *acrimony*, the old man found himself lonely and friendless.
syn: resentment, rancor, unkindness *ant*: amiability, tenderness, kindness

6. **adamant** (ăd′ ə mănt) *adj.* unyielding; firm in opinion
Despite the protests of the entire city council, the mayor remained *adamant*.
syn: stubborn *ant*: amenable, flexible

7. **adulation** (ăj ōō lā′ shən) *noun* excessive praise or admiration
She despised the *adulation* heaped on rock stars by young fans.
syn: flattery, adoration *ant*: derision, mockery

8. **affable** (ăf′ ə bel) *adj.* friendly; courteous; agreeable in manner; easy to talk to
The *affable* old man never lacked visitors.
syn: amiable, good-natured *ant*: disagreeable, irritable, bad-tempered

9. **agnostic** (ăg nŏs′ tĭk) *noun* one who believes that the existence of God is unknown and unknowable
Although he would not say there was no God, he did not attend church because he was an *agnostic*.

10. **agrarian** (ə grâr′ ē ən) *adj.* having to do with farms, farmers, or the use of land
Because New Jersey is mostly *agrarian*, it is called "The Garden State."
syn: agricultural, rural, pastoral *ant*: urban

Exercise I Words in Context

Fill in the blanks with the correct vocabulary words needed to complete the sentences.

acquitted **abhorred** **abetting** **abate**

A. Having been betrayed by a friend in his youth, the hermit ________________ mankind and kept mostly to himself. One dark night, after a storm that had raged for hours began to ________________, he was surprised by a knock on his door. It was a man who had just escaped from a nearby prison. The lonely old man fed and clothed the stranger and gave him a place to sleep. The next morning, however, he was awakened by the police who arrested him for ________________ an escaped convict. Had the old man not acted typically unpleasant at his trial, he probably would have been ________________.

affable **agnostic** **adulation** **acrimony** **agrarian** **adamant**

B. The mayor and the city council had debated for weeks on the rezoning issue. The councilmen were in favor of urbanizing, but the mayor insisted on maintaining the ________________ nature of the county. Despite the well-planned arguments of the councilmen, the mayor remained ________________ and refused to change his position.

C. The school board meeting began pleasantly enough with people exchanging ________________ greetings. However, once the issue of school prayer was raised, friendliness changed to ________________. Mr. Johnson, an ________________,who once had received a great deal of ________________ in the community for his work with troubled children, was the object of many attacks.

Exercise II Roots, Prefixes, and Suffixes

Study the entries and answer the questions that follow.

The prefix *mal–* means "bad, evil."
The root *bene* means "good."
The root *dict* means "to speak."

1. Without using a dictionary, try to define the following words:
   malevolent
   benevolent
   malediction
   benediction
   malefactor
   benefactor

2. After a biopsy, tumors are generally labeled ________________ or ________________.

3. List as many other related words as you can that begin with either *mal–* or *bene*.

Exercise III Usage Inferences

Choose the answer that best suits the situation.

1. Who would most likely *abhor* the thought of a math test tomorrow?
   A. the teacher who was sick and used an old test that allowed some students to cheat
   B. the student who felt that he knew math better than he understood English
   C. the group of students who studied together all week at each other's houses
   D. the student who spent no time studying because a new video game just came out

2. Which situation will most likely include *acrimony*?
   A. people playing cards for many hours with one person usually losing
   B. a dog and cat hissing and barking when they meet for the first time
   C. a divorce in which neither person will relinquish the house to the other
   D. an argument between teams in a soccer game after the referee missed a call

3. What is most *adamant*?
   A. a rock
   B. a stream
   C. anger
   D. travel

Exercise IV Reading Comprehension

Read the selection and answer the questions.

Let us suppose, therefore, that the government is entirely at one with the people and never thinks of exerting any power of coercion unless in agreement with what it conceives to be their voice. But I deny the right of the people to exercise such coercion, either by themselves or by their government. The power itself is illegitimate; the best government has no more title to it than the worst. It is noxious, or more noxious, when exerted in accordance with public opinion, than when in opposition to it. If all mankind, minus one, were of one opinion and only one person were of the contrary opinion, mankind would be no more justified in silencing that one person, than he, if he had the power, would be justified in silencing mankind.

–*John Stuart Mill*

1. The writer of this selection is primarily concerned about
   A. a government of the people.
   B. the abuse of power.
   C. justice for all.
   D. censorship.
   E. men and nations.

2. The word *noxious* in the fifth sentence means
   A. helpful.
   B. harmful.
   C. silly.
   D. important.
   E. peaceful.

3. The author states or implies that if the majority of people agree on one point,
   A. then the minority who disagree should keep silent.
   B. that in no way gives the majority the right to silence the minority.
   C. that is how democracy works.
   D. that is bad for the entire country.
   E. that a few people should not be allowed to disrupt things for everyone else.

4. The author contends or implies that
   A. when the government is entirely at one with the people, only then can it exert coercion.
   B. only the best of governments (i.e., the most democratic) has the right to control the speech of its citizens.
   C. no government has the right, under any circumstances, to control the speech of its citizens.
   D. if only one or a few voices disagree, they may be silenced.
   E. if the government and public opinion agree, only then can disagreements be silenced.

Lesson Two

1. **altercation** (ôl tər kā′ shən) *noun* a heated argument
As a result of the mounting tension, an *altercation* between the police and the residents broke out.
syn: controversy, quarrel, contention *ant*: harmony, agreement

2. **ambivalent** (ăm bĭv′ ə lənt) *adj.* being uncertain; unable to decide between two opposing points of view
He felt *ambivalent* about his job; although he hated the pressure, he loved the challenge.
syn: indecisive *ant*: opinionated, decisive

3. **amicable** (ăm′ ĭ kə bəl) *adj.* friendly; peaceable
After years of arguing, the two sides put down their weapons and came to an *amicable* agreement.
syn: agreeable, amiable *ant*: quarrelsome, warlike

4. **anathema** (ə năth′ ə mə) *noun* something that is disliked, cursed; a person cursed
Because they saw him as a traitor, his presence in town was *anathema* to the townspeople.
syn: abomination, abhorrence *ant*: blessing

5. **apathy** (ăp′ ə thē) *noun* lack of interest
Because of the *apathy* of its citizens, the town went from bad to worse.
syn: lethargy, unconcern, indifference *ant*: zeal, fervor

6. **appease** (ə pēz′) *verb* to make calm or quiet; to give in to the demands of
The small snack before dinner did nothing to *appease* his appetite.
syn: pacify, placate, allay *ant*: aggravate, defy

7. **arduous** (är′ jōō əs) *adj.* difficult; requiring much effort; strenuous
Refinishing the old bookcase proved to be an *arduous* task, though the finished product was well worth it.
syn: laborious *ant*: facile, easy, simple

8. **audacity** (ô dăs′ ĭ tē) *noun* insolence; rude boldness
The student's *audacity* in talking back to the teacher earned him a detention.
syn: effrontery, presumption, impudence *ant*: decorum, propriety, timidness

9. **augment** (ôg mĕnt′) *verb* to enlarge; to increase in amount or intensity
I had to take a second job to *augment* my income.
syn: expand, enhance *ant*: abate, shrivel, reduce

10. **austere** (ô stēr′) *adj.* stern, severe; plain
The sober, old judge was as *austere* in his manner as he was in his lifestyle and dress.
syn: abstemious, rigorous, ascetic *ant*: luxurious, affable, indulgent

Exercise I Words in Context

Fill in the blanks with the correct vocabulary words needed to complete the sentences.

anathema **amicable** **ambivalent** **altercation**

A. The two friends shared similar interests and, for a long time, had enjoyed an ____________________ relationship. One time, however, the younger friend suggested a trip to the mountains, and the older friend hesitated. He felt ____________________ because he wanted to go to the mountains, but he also wanted to go to the beach. The disagreement that followed resulted in a bitter ____________________. Now the younger friend regards the older as ____________________ and will not even speak when they meet on the street.

apathy **audacity** **austere** **augment** **arduous** **appease**

B. The Puritans led a very ____________________ lifestyle. The hard, rocky soil made farming a most ____________________ task. Because their supply of stored goods sometimes ran very low, they depended on a good harvest to ____________________ their food supply.

C. Tom was a timid boy, but when one of his teachers mistook his quiet reserve for ____________________ and ordered Tom to pay attention, his forthright response to her bordered on ____________________. It took the principal some time to ____________________ both angry parties.

Exercise II Roots, Prefixes, and Suffixes

Study the entries and answer the questions that follow.

The root *anthro* means "man."
The suffix *–ology* means "study of."
The root *theo* means "god," "religion."

1. Without using a dictionary, try to define the following words:

   anthropology
   anthropomorphic
   theology
   atheism
   anthropoid
   theocracy

2. What is *sociology* the study of?

3. List as many words as you can think of that begin with either *anthro* or *theo* or end in *–ology*.

Exercise III Usage Inferences

Choose the answer that best suits the situation.

1. Which group of words would most likely describe something that is *austere*?
   A. tasty, properly cooked, and perfectly seasoned
   B. not funny, long, dull, and boring to read
   C. colorless, bleak, cheap looking, and undecorated
   D. confusing, complicated, difficult, and opinionated

2. Who would be least likely to be *apathetic* about money?
   A. a bored student
   B. a fine actor
   C. a business owner
   D. an elderly mayor

3. Which is the most physically *arduous*?
   A. running a marathon
   B. studying for a test
   C. walking through a zoo
   D. babysitting for twins

Exercise IV Reading Comprehension

Read the selection and answer the questions.

Life has never been a May-game for men: throughout time the lot of the dumb millions born to toil has been defaced with suffering, injustices, and heavy burdens; not play at all, but hard work has made the sinews and the heart sore. As slaves, and even as dukes and kings, men have often been made weary of their life. They said, behold, it is not sport. Life is a grim business and our backs can bear no more. And yet, I venture to believe that in no time since the beginning of society has the lot of millions been as unbearable as it is today. It is not to die, or even to die of hunger, that makes a man wretched; all men must die. But it is to live miserable and not know why; to work hard and yet gain nothing; to be heart-worn, weary yet isolated; to die slowly all our life long, imprisoned in a dead, dead, infinite injustice; this is what is intolerable and causes revolutions.

–Thomas Carlyle

1. The phrase *dumb millions* refers to the
   A. uneducated people in the country.
   B. people who can neither speak nor hear.
   C. poor people in the country.
   D. people who do not share Carlyle's opinion of the government.
   E. immigrants in the country.

2. The author contends that the men of his time are miserable because they
   A. are starving to death.
   B. know they are going to die young.
   C. are suffering many injustices.
   D. have no one to love.
   E. have lost their faith in God.

3. The author implies that the situation may result in
   A. millions of people starving to death.
   B. people rising in revolt.
   C. a dictator taking over the country.
   D. a complete breakdown of authority.
   E. All of the above are correct.

4. The author states that life for the working man
   A. has constantly been improving.
   B. is much worse now than it has been in the past.
   C. is pretty much the same.
   D. is improved through hard work.
   E. is improved through prayer and good works.

Lesson Three

1. **avarice** (ăv′ ə rĭs) *noun* excessive greed; desire for wealth
He became a doctor not to save lives but to appease his *avarice*.
syn: cupidity *ant*: liberality, generosity

2. **avid** (ă vĭd′) *adj.* eager; extremely interested
He was such an *avid* moviegoer that the theater gave him a half-priced, lifetime pass.
syn: voracious, keen *ant*: apathetic

3. **bacchanalian** (băk ə nāl′ yən) *adj.* wild drunkenness
Alcohol was not sold at the event because the planners did not want it to become a *bacchanalian* party.

4. **balk** (bôk) *verb* to stop short and refuse to continue; to obstruct
Although he desperately needed the money, he *balked* at the idea of working for less than minimum wage.
syn: hesitate, frustrate, block *ant*: facilitate, abet

5. **banter** (băn′ tər) *noun* teasing; good-natured joking
As she sat at the table, Ruth enjoyed listening to the *banter* of her husband and his old college roommate.

6. **barrister** (băr′ ĭ stər) *noun* a lawyer
In England, a lawyer or attorney who argues cases in court is called a *barrister*.

7. **bask** (băsk) *verb* to lie in or be exposed to warmth; to enjoy something pleasant
While in Florida on vacation, all she did was *bask* in the sun.

8. **bastion** (băs′ chən) *noun* a strong defense; a fort
During critical times in the history of the world, the United States has been called the *bastion* of democracy.

9. **bawdy** (bô′ dē) *adj.* indecent; humorously obscene
Because some people called it a *bawdy* show, the car manufacturer withdrew as a sponsor for the program.
syn: risqué

10. **befuddle** (bĭ fŭd′ l) *verb* to confuse; to perplex
Did he try to *befuddle* you with his fast talk?
syn: bewilder, fluster *ant*: clarify

Exercise I Words in Context

Fill in the blanks with the correct vocabulary words needed to complete the sentences.

bacchanalian **avid** **avarice** **banter**

A. Although he had a good salary, he was driven to steal the money out of pure ________________. In prison, although he initially enjoyed the ________________ of the other inmates, he soon became bored with the stories of their former ________________ lifestyles. Thus, while in prison, he became a(n) ________________ reader.

balk **bawdy** **bask** **befuddled** **bastion** **barrister**

B. By winning this particularly tough case, which dealt with British maritime law, the ________________ hoped to be able to ________________ in the praises of his fellow lawyers.

C. When the show originally opened thirty years ago, the ________________ language offended many people. Today, most people walk away from the show ________________ by the controversy that once surrounded it.

D. The judge expected the reporter to not only ________________ at divulging his news sources, but also repeat the judge's lecture about America being a ________________ of free speech.

Exercise II Roots, Prefixes, and Suffixes

Study the entries and answer the questions that follow.

The root *aud* means "hear."
The root *cis/cide* means "cut," "kill."
The root *vis/vid* means "see."
The suffix *–ible/able* means "able."

1. Without using a dictionary, try to define the following words:

   audible
   vista
   visionary
   auditory
   herbicide
   incision

2. In the word *suicide* the root *sui* probably means ________________.

3. List as many words as you can that have the roots *aud, vis,* or *vid* in them.

4. An *incisive* comment is one that is ____________________.

5. List as many words as you can that end in *cide*.

Exercise III Usage Inferences

Choose the answer that best suits the situation.

1. *Avarice* might eventually lead to
   A. dancing.
   B. running.
   C. overeating.
   D. stealing.

2. Which sentence is the best example of *befuddlement*?
   A. I don't know what you are talking about.
   B. I don't know, and what's more, I don't care.
   C. I don't know, but I'll try to find out the answer.
   D. I don't know if I even care about what happens.

3. What would a *barrister* deal with?
   A. pets
   B. arguments
   C. vehicles
   D. laws

Exercise IV Reading Comprehension

Read the selection and answer the questions.

A foolish consistency is the hobgoblin of little minds that is adored by little statesmen, philosophers and divines. With consistency, a great soul has simply nothing to do. He may as well concern himself with his shadow on the wall. Speak what you think now in hard words and tomorrow speak what tomorrow thinks in hard words again, though it contradict every thing you said today. You are sure to be misunderstood, but is it so bad then to be misunderstood? Pythagoras was misunderstood, and Socrates, and Jesus, and Luther, and Copernicus, and Galileo, and Newton, and every pure and wise spirit that ever took flesh.

–Ralph Waldo Emerson

1. The first sentence suggests that
   A. consistency is to be valued.
   B. consistency is not always necessary.
   C. only people with small minds value foolish consistency.
   D. Both B and C are correct.
   E. All of the above are correct.

2. The author suggests that if a man is inconsistent in his statements,
   A. people will have little faith in him.
   B. people may misunderstand him.
   C. he will become great.
   D. he will understand the great philosophers.
   E. he will never be able to understand the great philosophers.

3. The author states or implies that
   A. we will be both happier and wiser if we think through our feelings.
   B. each day brings us new thoughts, and the thoughts we have today may contradict thoughts of yesterday.
   C. some of the great minds of the past believed in spiritual values.
   D. "like shadows on the wall," we never see reality directly.
   E. most statesmen, philosophers, and divines do value inconsistency.

4. The author's main point in this selection is that
   A. greatness is often misunderstood.
   B. speaking the truth can be dangerous.
   C. consistency is necessary for logical thinking.
   D. consistency is much admired by little minds.
   E. we should speak the truth as we see it even at the risk of being inconsistent.

Lesson Four

1. **bigot** (bĭg′ ət) *noun* one who is intolerant of another's beliefs, opinions, or values
The *bigot* is the worst enemy of democracy and free speech.

2. **cajole** (kə jōl′) *verb* to persuade with promises and flattery
Despite his best efforts, the mayor could not *cajole* Colonel Harris into donating the land to the city.
syn: coax, wheedle *ant*: dissuade, deter

3. **candid** (kăn′ dĭd) *adj.* outspoken, blunt; straightforward, honest
He gave a *candid* speech about the time he had spent in prison.
syn: sincere, open *ant*: evasive, equivocal

4. **canine** (kā′ nīn) *adj.* having to do with dogs; *noun* a dog
Many police departments have *canine* units with dogs trained to sniff out drugs and bombs.

5. **capricious** (kə prĭsh′ əs) *adj.* guided by whim rather than reason; impulsive
After planning his camping trip to the mountains for months, he made a *capricious* decision to go to the seashore.
syn: fickle, erratic *ant*: steadfast, undeviating

6. **castigate** (kăs′ tĭ gāt) *verb* to criticize or punish for the purpose of correction
The parson *castigated* the young boy for sleeping in church.
syn: chastise, discipline, reprimand *ant*: commend, laud, praise

7. **caustic** (kô′ stĭk) *adj.* biting, sharp, severe, sarcastic; able to burn or corrode
Because of his *caustic* comments, his wife finally left him.
syn: tart, corrosive, harsh *ant*: mild, saccharine, gentle, easy-going

8. **chaos** (kā′ ŏs) *noun* complete disorder
The new teacher was given the job of ending the *chaos* and restoring order in the classroom.
syn: confusion, shambles *ant*: order, harmony

9. **charlatan** (shär′ lə tĕn) *noun* one who pretends to have more knowledge or skill than he or she really has
Many of the supposed medical men of the Old West with their miracle drugs were really no more than *charlatans*.
syn: quack, impostor, fraud, fake

10. **chastise** (chăs′ tīz) *verb* to punish severely
After Kristen had skipped two rehearsals, the director of the play *chastised* her by giving her a smaller role.
syn: reprove, discipline *ant*: reward, comfort

Exercise I Words in Context

Fill in the blanks with the correct vocabulary words needed to complete the sentences.

caustic **charlatan** **candid** **castigate**

A. When the salesman was discovered to be a ________________, angry customers made ________________ comments on his website to ________________ him for taking advantage of them. In a surprisingly ________________ response, he posted an acknowledgment and apology. He also issued refunds, but that did not prevent police from charging him with fraud.

cajole **chastise** **bigot** **chaos** **capricious** **canine**

B. The shop owner tried to ________________ the tourist into buying a locally made necklace by offering to give her a discount if she also bought the matching earrings. When the tourist declined, saying that she buys jewelry made only in her own country, the owner accused her of being a ________________.

C. The ________________ and Feline Clubs held a joint fundraiser to benefit the local animal shelter. Everything was going well until one dog owner let his pet, Bonzo, off the leash. The room erupted into ________________ as the playful dog chased the cats, who ran in every direction. Fortunately, Bonzo was caught before too much damage was done, but the organizers decided to ________________ the owner for his ________________ action by asking him to leave the event.

Exercise II Roots, Prefixes, and Suffixes

Study the entries and answer the questions that follow.

The root *alter* means "change," "other."
The root *ego* means "I."
The root *mega* means "large."
The root *polis* means "city," "state."

1. Without using a dictionary, write a definition for each of the following words:

   megalopolis
   metropolitan
   alteration
   egotist
   alter ego
   egocentric

2. A person who is a *megalomaniac* has a mental disorder characterized by delusions of ____________________.

3. If you *alter* your plans, you ____________________ ___.

4. List as many words as you can think of that begin with the root *ego* or *mega*.

Exercise III Usage Inferences

Choose the answer that best suits the situation.

1. What can you correctly assume about *bigots*?
   A. They like each other regardless of what happens.
   B. They dislike people who are different from them.
   C. They act primarily out of a love for their country.
   D. They all have the same ideas about race and gender.

2. What is an example of being *chastised*?
   A. Put down that knife before you hurt someone.
   B. Please do not say anything else negative about me.
   C. You will probably get a very serious punishment for that.
   D. Your curfew is now 9:30 because of what you did last night.

3. In what situation would *chaos* probably occur?
   A. after a tornado struck a town
   B. after a football game happened
   C. after an epidemic was stopped
   D. after a store was robbed

Exercise IV Reading Comprehension

Read the selection and answer the questions.

One only has to go back several generations, to find a time when the household was practically the center in which were carried on, or about which were clustered, all the typical forms of industrial occupation. The clothing worn was for the most part made in the house; the members of the household were usually familiar also with the shearing of the sheep, the carding and spinning of the wool, and the plying of the loom. Instead of pressing a button and flooding the house with electric light, the whole process of getting illumination was followed in its toilsome length from the killing of the animal and the frying of fat, to the making of wicks and dipping of candles. The supply of flour, of lumber, of foods, of building materials, of household furniture, even of metal ware, of nails, hinges, hammers, etc., was produced in the immediate neighborhood, in shops which were constantly open to inspection and often centers of the neighborhood congregation. The entire industrial process stood revealed, from the production on the farm of the raw materials, till the finished article was actually put to use. Not only this, but practically every member of the household had his own share in the work. The children, as they gained in strength and capacity, were gradually initiated into the mysteries of the several processes. It was a matter of immediate and personal concern, even to the point of actual participation. As such, the educative forces were constantly operative.

–John Dewey

1. The last sentence suggests that the education of earlier generations was
   A. better than the education children get today.
   B. not as good as the education children get today.
   C. immediate and continually in operation in daily life.
   D. much cheaper and much more effective than education today.
   E. neither cost-effective nor a good education.

2. The author states or implies that
   A. education was less important in earlier times.
   B. man lost control of his own life.
   C. children today do not grow up observing many of the things their forefathers had.
   D. in early times, families were happier because they were closer.
   E. in early times, children were exploited and forced to fill adult roles.

3. The author's main point in this selection is that
   A. not everything that changes always changes for the best.
   B. education is where you find it.
   C. we have to look back only a few generations to see how much the world has changed.
   D. in early times, children were educated by observing and participating in daily life.
   E. the child's role in society has changed for the better.

4. The author implies that
   A. it is inappropriate for industry to be open to public scrutiny and interference.
   B. it is preferable for goods to be made locally and in plain view of the public.
   C. people resented having to make their own clothing and create their own lighting.
   D. being involved in the processes of daily living was too difficult for children.
   E. it is just as important for children to play as it is to do household chores.

Lesson Five

VOCABULARY *for the* College Bound

1. **circumspect** (sûr′ kəm spĕkt) *adj.* careful, watchful, cautious
It is a good idea to be *circumspect* of buying a previously owned computer.
syn: wary, prudent *ant:* rash, foolhardy

2. **circumvent** (sûr kəm vĕnt′) *verb* to bypass or go around; to avoid by cleverness
Although he did not tell a lie, he did *circumvent* my question by claiming that he could not remember what happened the night before.
syn: evade *ant:* abet, facilitate, promote

3. **clandestine** (klăn dĕs′ tĭn) *adj.* secret
Romeo and Juliet were forced to hold *clandestine* meetings because of their parents' feud.
syn: covert, furtive, underhanded *ant:* forthright, open

4. **clement** (klĕm′ ənt) *adj.* merciful, lenient; mild
Despite the abhorrent nature of the crime, the judge handed down a surprisingly *clement* sentence.
syn: benign, temperate *ant:* harsh, severe

5. **cliché** (klē shā′) *noun* a worn-out idea or overused expression
While the candidate had promised new ideas, he soon began to use the same old *clichés*.
syn: platitude

6. **coerce** (kō ûrs′) *verb* to force a person to do something against his or her will
People sometimes feel *coerced* to do something because of peer pressure.
syn: compel, constrain, force

7. **collaborate** (kə lăb′ ə rāt) *verb* 1. to work with another toward a goal
2. to cooperate with an enemy invader
   1. The lyricist and composer *collaborated* on the stage musical.
   2. Although he did not have the courage to actively oppose the Nazis, he did not *collaborate* with them.

syn: 1. cooperate 2. abet

8. **comely** (kŭm′ lē) *adj.* attractive or handsome; pleasing to the sight
The writer would often refer to his beautiful heroine as a "*comely* lass."
ant: homely, repulsive, plain

9. **complacent** (kəm plā′ sənt) *adj.* pleased with oneself or one's deeds
Though he was friendly, Al tended to be a little too *complacent* for me.
syn: unconcerned, conceited, contented *ant:* discontented, humble

10. **concur** (kən kûr′) *verb* to be of the same opinion; to agree with
He said that three hours was too long for a lecture, and we all *concurred.*
syn: approve, assent *ant:* disagree, demur, dissent

Exercise I Words in Context

Fill in the blanks with the correct vocabulary words needed to complete the sentences.

cliché **circumvent** **clandestine** **clement** **circumspect**

A. Although the reporter wanted to be the first to break the story, he also wanted to keep his source confidential. It was for this reason that he arranged the ______________ meeting near the waterfront. In the middle of a bridge, he changed taxis in order to ______________ anyone who might want to follow him. As he walked the final block to his destination, he looked at the bright moon and stars and was grateful for the ______________ weather which would make this interview much easier. There was one man standing under the street light when he arrived. "A stitch in time saves nine," he whispered hoarsely. This ______________ was the agreed upon password. The man, after making a slow and ______________ survey of the area, replied, "Get out your notebook; I'm ready to tell you the whole story."

comely **coerce** **concurred** **complacent** **collaborate**

B. Though the two had long been friendly, they had never been able to ______________ on a production for the stage. The poet was a little too ______________ about his own small successes to even consider working with someone else, and the composer knew it would be foolish to try to ______________ him to work together. Finally, however, their agent offered a deal with a ______________ salary and benefit package. He said they could not afford to pass up the opportunity; they ______________. The result was a hit stage musical that made them both wealthy.

Exercise II Roots, Prefixes, and Suffixes

Study the entries and answer the questions that follow.

The prefix *circum–* means "around, on all sides."
The prefix *intro–* means "in, within, inside of."
The root *spec/spect* means "to see, look at."
The root *vert/vers* means "to turn."

1. Without using a dictionary, write a definition for each of the following words:

   circumnavigate
   introspect
   retrospect
   circumlocutions
   introvert
   extrovert

2. List as many words as you can think of that contain the roots *spec*, *spect*, *vert*, or *vers*. Try to define each word literally.

3. List as many words as you can think of that contain the prefix *circum* or the prefix *intro–*. Try to define each word literally.

Exercise III Usage Inferences

Choose the answer that best suits the situation.

1. A person who is *circumspect* would most likely be someone who
   A. dislikes his or her neighbors.
   B. picks his or her friends carefully.
   C. confides in his or her parents.
   D. pretends to be interested in science.

2. Which is an example of a *cliché*?
   A. Believe what you want to believe.
   B. This is an amazing novel to read.
   C. I was scared out of my wits yesterday.
   D. The dog ate his dinner all the time.

3. Who is most likely to be *complacent* about a trophy?
   A. the person who actually made it
   B. the person who never won it
   C. the person who won it last year
   D. the person who won it three years ago

Exercise IV Reading Comprehension

Read the selection and answer the questions.

Man is timid and apologetic; he is no longer upright; he dares not say "I think, I am," but quotes some saint or sage. He is ashamed before the blade of grass or the blowing rose. These roses under my willow make no reference to former roses or to better ones; they are what they are: they exist with God today. There is no time to them. There is simply the rose; it is perfect in every moment of its existence. Its nature is satisfied and it satisfies nature in all moments alike. But man postpones or remembers; he does not live in the present, but with reverted eye laments the past, or, heedless of the riches that surround him, stands on tiptoe to foresee the future. He cannot be happy and strong until he too lives with nature in the present, above time.

–Ralph Waldo Emerson

1. In the first sentence the author suggests that
   A. Man does not think for himself.
   B. Man relies on the authority of others for his thoughts.
   C. Man is not afraid to think for himself.
   D. Man does not understand nature.
   E. A, B, and C are correct.

2. The author states or implies that
   A. God is unhappy with us.
   B. man is a nervous, fearful creature.
   C. man should stand up for his rights.
   D. man should show reverence for God and nature.
   E. man is slowly getting better.

3. The author's main point in this selection is that
   A. man is a timid and apologetic creature.
   B. man must live with nature in the present.
   C. man is always postponing his life.
   D. nature is more perfect than man.
   E. God will show man the correct way.

4. What comparison is the author making in the essay?
   A. He compares nature to God.
   B. He compares love to nature.
   C. He compares humanity and nature.
   D. He compares nature to perfection.
   E. He compares various types of nature with each other.

Lesson Six

1. **condone** (kən dōn′) *verb* to forgive or overlook an offense by treating the wrongdoer as if there had been nothing wrong
After they had heard about the man's starving family, many people found it easy to *condone* his stealing the food.
syn: pardon, excuse, acquit *ant*: condemn, indict, avenge

2. **connive** (kə nīv′) *verb* to cooperate secretly in a wrongdoing
Although the judge claimed to have fought against corruption, many people believe that he *connived* with crooked politicians in order to make himself rich.
syn: collaborate, conspire

3. **connoisseur** (kŏn ə sûr′) *noun* an expert; an authority
The chef watched nervously as the *connoisseur* tasted the soup.
syn: critic *ant*: novice, beginner, amateur

4. **contrite** (kən trīt′) *adj.* showing regret and sorrow, usually for having committed some wrongdoing
After she was told to be quiet, Jennifer became *contrite* and did not act up in class again.
syn: repentant, remorseful, penitent *ant*: obdurate, shameless

5. **copious** (kō′ pē əs) *adj.* abundant; large in number or quantity
At the city council meeting, the complaints were *copious*, but the suggestions were few.
syn: profuse, bountiful, plentiful *ant*: meager, sparse, scanty

6. **crass** (krăs) *adj.* coarse, stupid, tasteless
The comment you made about how dirty his house looked was *crass* and uncalled for.
syn: crude, obtuse, graceless *ant*: suave, polished, refined

7. **credence** (krēd′ ns) *noun* belief or trust
The father gave *credence* to the boy's story about the fight.
syn: credit, faith *ant*: distrust, skepticism, doubt

8. **culinary** (kŭl′ ə nĕr′ ē) *adj* having to do with the kitchen or cooking
Most famous chefs are graduates of great schools of *culinary* arts.

9. **culmination** (kŭl mə nā′ shən) *noun* the apex, highest point; completion, finish
Graduation marks the *culmination* of formal schooling.
syn: end, finale, climax *ant*: beginning

10. **cult** (kŭlt) *noun* a fad-like devotion to a person, thing, or idea; a group of people bound together by the same thing, person, or ideal
In order to join the *cult*, the recruits had to shave their heads and walk over broken glass.
syn: sect

Exercise I Words in Context

Fill in the blanks with the correct vocabulary words needed to complete the sentences.

connoisseur **connived** **contrite** **copious** **condone**

A. The police said that the accused criminal had ________________ with others to swindle people out of money. His illegal skill had brought him ________________ material rewards, and the newspaper headlines referred to him as a "________________ of Cons." Although he had been arrested many times, he had always managed to find a judge willing to release him. Finally, however, he was sent before a stern judge who found it impossible to ________________ his criminal activities. Since there was no evidence that the criminal felt at all ________________ for his actions, the judge sentenced him to the maximum number of years in prison.

crass **culinary** **credence** **cult** **culmination**

B. The young man knew he had the power to persuade people to action, so he began to teach his philosophy to anyone who would listen. He was a persuasive speaker, and many people soon gave ________________ to what he said about food and health. Soon, he had a small band of followers who designed uniforms for themselves and became something similar to a ________________.

C. Tension mounted until it reached its ________________ on the steps of the school for ________________ arts, where students threw stale muffins at the ________________ people who made insulting comments about the school and its students.

Exercise II Roots, Prefixes, and Suffixes

Study the entries and answer the questions that follow.

The root *arch* means "rule," "govern," "to be first."
The root *dem/demos* means "people."
The root *mit/mis* means "send."
The suffix *–ist* means "one who practices or believes."
The suffix *–crat* means "rule by."

1. Without using a dictionary, write a definition for the following words:

   archetype
   demography
   transmit
   monarchy
   democracy
   remit

2. A *technocrat* would be a supporter of __________________________________.

3. The root *oligos* means few; therefore, an *oligarchy* would probably be ____________________.

4. List as many words as you can think of that contain the roots *arch, dem/demos,* and *mit/mis,* or the suffix *–crat.*

5. The prefix *ana–* means "without," or "against"; therefore, an *anarchist* is ____________________.

Exercise III Usage Inferences

Choose the answer that best suits the situation.

1. What would a good pet owner not *condone*?
   A. not playing with a dog
   B. not feeding a cat
   C. taking a dog on walks
   D. taking a cat to the vet

2. Which item in a house is an example of something relating to the word *culinary*?
   A. a stove
   B. a stairway
   C. a bathroom
   D. an air conditioner

3. Which emotion goes best with the meaning of *contrite*?
   A. happy
   B. sad
   C. angry
   D. sorry

Exercise IV Reading Comprehension

Read the selection and answer the questions.

The child lives in a somewhat narrow world of personal contacts. Things hardly come within his experience unless they touch, intimately and obviously, his own well-being, or that of his family and friends. His world is a world of persons with their personal interests, rather than a realm of facts and laws. Not truth, in the sense of conformity to external fact, but affection and sympathy, is its keynote. As against this, the course of study met in the school presents material stretching back indefinitely in time, and extending outward indefinitely into space. The child is taken out of his familiar physical environment, hardly more than a square mile or so in area, into the wide world—yes, and even to the bounds of the solar system.

–*John Dewey*

1. The author's main point in this selection is that
   A. affection and sympathy are more important than knowledge.
   B. schools sometimes do more harm than good.
   C. education expands a child's knowledge by opening the world.
   D. the solar system is infinite.
   E. there is a need for more home education.

2. The author states or implies that
   A. the school course of study expands a child's mind.
   B. a young child's experience with the world is limited.
   C. affection and sympathy are more important to the young child than truth, in the sense of conformity to external facts.
   D. All of the above are correct.
   E. None of the above are correct.

3. From this selection, we might infer that the author
   A. has no children of his own.
   B. has studied children and the way they learn.
   C. has no great love of children.
   D. is impatient with the ways that schools teach young children.
   E. expects everyone to disagree with him.

4. The author's tone in this passage is
   A. angry.
   B. excited.
   C. wistful.
   D. gloomy.
   E. informational.

Lesson Seven

1. **cynical** (sĭn′ ĭ kəl) *adj.* inclined to distrust or deny the goodness or sincerity of human motives
A *cynical* person frequently encounters problems because others cannot trust his or her words.
syn: distrustful, skeptical, scornful *ant:* idealistic, optimistic

2. **decorum** (dĭ kôr′ əm) *noun* conformity to accepted standards of conduct; proper behavior
The man, who was a belligerent atheist, acted with surprising *decorum* during the church service.
syn: propriety, dignity, etiquette *ant:* impropriety, inappropriateness

3. **demagogue** (dĕm′ ə gôg) *noun* a leader who appeals to the emotions and prejudices of people, especially to advance his or her own power
Once the leader of the revolt defeated the dictator, he then became a *demagogue*.
syn: agitator, rabble-rouser

4. **demure** (dĭ myŏŏr′) *adj.* quiet and modest, not showy or gaudy
On stage, Jesse dressed like an evil king, but at home he wore *demure*, bland colors.
syn: decorous, reserved *ant:* audacious, conceited, blunt

5. **deprecate** (dĕp′ rĭ kāt) *verb* to express disapproval of; to depreciate one's effort
Because the others *deprecated* his earlier ideas, he offered no new ones.
syn: belittle, disparage *ant:* approve, commend, praise

6. **destitute** (dĕs′ tĭ tōōt) *adj.* extremely poor; lacking necessities like food and shelter
Since they had no insurance, the fire, which completely destroyed their home, left them *destitute*.
syn: indigent, impoverished, penniless *ant:* opulent, affluent

7. **diffident** (dĭf′ ĭ dənt) *adj.* lacking in self-confidence; shy
After hearing of the man's accomplishments, it was especially hard to understand his *diffident* attitude.
syn: timid, modest *ant:* arrogant, aggressive, forward

8. **dilemma** (dĭ lĕm′ ə) *noun* a difficult choice; especially a choice between two equally undesirable alternatives
Whether I should repair my old car or purchase a new one presented me with a real *dilemma*.
syn: quandary, plight, predicament

9. **dilettante** (dĭl′ ĭ tänt) *noun* one who studies an art or science for mere amusement
Though just a *dilettante*, Karl practiced his piano with as much diligence as a concert pianist.
syn: amateur, dabbler *ant*: expert, professional

10. **disparity** (dĭ spăr′ ĭ tē) *noun* inequality; difference
He was forty and she twenty, but their marriage was very happy despite the *disparity* in their ages.
syn: disproportion, dissimilarity *ant*: parity, likeness, equality

Exercise I Words in Context

Fill in the blanks with the correct vocabulary words needed to complete the sentences.

demagogue **demure** **decorum** **cynical** **deprecated**

A. The citizens of the small kingdom had lived for years under the rule of a foolish and weak king. That summer, however, a leader arose among them. Although the king called the young man a __________________, who only wished to arouse the people with exaggerations and lies, the young man conducted himself with the greatest __________________ in order that his behavior could not be criticized.

B. Because he was a __________________, almost shy man who expressed a __________________ distrust for all politicians, it surprised everyone when he agreed to run for public office. After winning and taking office, however, he also had his critics. Despite all he had done for the people, there were citizens who __________________ much of what he had accomplished.

disparity **diffident** **destitute** **dilemma** **dilettante**

C. Mrs. Tate looked at the young man who stood before her. Although his resume and job application showed him to be a well-qualified candidate, he stood in front of the desk, eyes staring at the carpet and seemed surprisingly __________________. What Mrs. Tate didn't know, however, was that the young man told lies on his application. After he was hired, though, she learned about the __________________ between the application and the man's actual work experience, and she was faced with a serious __________________: fire a very good worker or overlook the lies on his application.

D. While a rich __________________ may spend his life studying whatever pleases him without any thought of the future, the poorer man who devotes his life to art may very well end up __________________ in his old age.

Exercise II Roots, Prefixes, and Suffixes

Study the entries and answer the questions that follow.

The root *fid* means "faith," "trust."
The root *form* means "shape."
The suffix *–tion* means "the act of."
The prefix *re–* means "back," "again."

1. Without using a dictionary, write a definition for each of the following words:

   reformation
   creationist
   reverted
   fidelity
   malformed
   confide

2. *Fidelity* is ______________________________.

3. The Marine Corps motto "*Semper Fidelis*" means ____________________.

4. List as many words as you can think of that contain the roots *fid* or *form*.

Exercise III Usage Inferences

Choose the answer that best suits the situation.

1. People who are *destitute*
   A. accept things as they are.
   B. don't have enough money.
   C. become used to their situation.
   D. are unusually happy.

2. Which is the best example of a *dilemma*?
   A. believing in Santa Claus or not believing in him
   B. playing in a game or watching the game
   C. paying the rent on the house or buying food
   D. reading a book or seeing the movie of it

3. The *disparity* in people's chances of winning the lottery would be least likely to involve
   A. the jobs they have.
   B. the luck they have.
   C. how many tickets they buy.
   D. how many times they play.

Exercise IV Reading Comprehension

Read the selection and answer the questions.

To question all things; to never turn away from any difficulty; to accept no doctrine either from ourselves or from other people without a rigid scrutiny by negative criticism; to allow no fallacy, or incoherence, or confusion of thought, step by unperceived, and above all, to insist upon having the meaning of a word clearly understood before using it, and the meaning of a proposition understood, before assenting to it; these are the lessons we learn from the ancient dialecticians.

–Ralph Waldo Emerson

1. The best restatement of the main idea of the passage is
   A. to question all things, never turning away from difficulty, and to accept no doctrine without first examining it with a negative criticism.
   B. to examine critically all propositions letting no fallacy, incoherence, or confusion of thought step by unperceived.
   C. to examine all propositions and insist upon having the meaning of a word clearly understood before using it and the meaning of a proposition before assenting to it.
   D. to examine critically everything we are told or hear and to question anything we think might be incorrect; clearly understand the meaning of a word before using it and totally understand the meaning of a statement before agreeing to it.
   E. None of the above are correct.

2. The author is encouraging students to
   A. listen to their parents and teachers.
   B. accept all authority.
   C. reject all authority.
   D. critically examine everything they are told.
   E. study diligently and do all their work.

3. We might infer from this statement that Emerson
   A. does not understand how a private school operates.
   B. does not take anyone's word for his authority.
   C. has studied with the ancient dialecticians.
   D. has a very negative attitude toward life.
   E. All of the above are correct.

4. The author states or implies that
   A. most or all doctrine is incorrect.
   B. most words are very vague.
   C. we should ask questions if we don't understand something.
   D. we should persevere until we clearly understand the point being made.
   E. Both C and D are correct.

Lesson Eight

1. **divulge** (dĭ vŭlj´) *verb* to reveal something private or secret
Divulging the contents of the top-secret document caused the reporter's arrest.
syn: uncover, unveil, disclose *ant:* cloak, veil, conceal

2. **docile** (dŏs´ əl) *adj.* easy to teach or manage
The dog was usually *docile*, but would growl if anyone took its favorite toy.
syn: submissive, compliant *ant:* headstrong, willful

3. **dogmatic** (dôg măt´ ĭk) *adj.* stating an opinion in an authoritative, superior, or arrogant manner
Because of the professor's *dogmatic* approach, the students were afraid to ask questions.
syn: dictatorial *ant:* humble, servile

4. **dole** (dōl) *verb* to distribute; to give out sparingly
Food was *doled* out carefully to people affected by the storm.
syn: apportion, measure

5. **dolorous** (dō´ lər əs) *adj.* mournful, sad
At first, the movie was slow and *dolorous*, but then came some car chases and explosions.
syn: sorrowful, painful *ant:* happy, joyful

6. **dour** (dour) *adj.* gloomy, sullen
The librarian's *dour* expression made students feel as if they had done something wrong.
syn: stern, severe *ant:* pleasant, happy

7. **droll** (drōl) *adj.* amusing in an odd way
He had a *droll* manner of telling stories that kept everyone entertained.
syn: funny, wry *ant:* dull, flat, boring

8. **duplicity** (dōō plĭs´ ĭ tē) *noun* intentional deceit in speech or conduct
She could forgive him for wanting to date other people, but she could not condone his *duplicity* in saying she was his only girlfriend.
syn: hypocrisy, deception *ant:* straightforwardness, honesty

9. **effigy** (ĕf´ ĭ jē) *noun* an image of a person or thing; usually a crude image of a hated person
During the anti-government march, protesters made a large *effigy* of the hated leader of the government, then burned it.
syn: representation, figure

10. **emaciated** (ĭ mā´ shē āt əd) *adj.* extremely thin, wasted away
The *emaciated* form of the starved prisoner was buried in the prisoner-of-war cemetery.
syn: shriveled, withered *ant:* plump, fattened

Exercise I Words in Context

Fill in the blanks with the correct vocabulary words needed to complete the sentences.

divulge **duplicity** **effigy** **docile** **dolorous**

A. The king's council had long been aware of the king's ________________, but they could not get enough evidence to convict him of any crime. The man had long been hated by the citizens of the country, but they were a(n) ________________ group that did not have the courage to remove him from the throne. One day, the Secretary of the Treasury overheard a conversation between the king and a wealthy businessman in the country. The press asked what had happened during the conversation, but the minister would not ________________ the information to anyone but the other members of the council. When this was done, they all went to the king's castle that night and burned the ________________ they had made of the king on his front lawn. Posting guards around the castle, they allowed no one to enter or leave. After several weeks the once-jovial king and his servants emerged looking very tired and ________________.

dogmatic **dour** **dole** **droll** **emaciated**

B. Early in life the minister had had a quick smile and a(n) ________________ sense of humor that made most people laugh. As he got older, however, he started to change. Previously, he had always tried to see the other person's point of view, his statements were now ________________. His once-bright personality now was ________________. He would no longer ________________ out candy to kids on holidays. Strangest of all was the physical change in him. Although he continued to eat well, each day he looked more and more ________________.

Exercise II Roots, Prefixes, and Suffixes

Study the entries and answer the questions that follow.

The root *frag/fract* means "break."
The root *chrono* means "time."
The suffix *–ment* means "the result of" or "product of the action."

1. Without using a dictionary, write a definition for each of the following words:
   chronic
   chronological
   fragment
   chronicle
   fragile
   refract

2. If a telephone rang during the play *Julius Caesar,* this would be an *anachronism* because it is ______________________________.

3. A *fragmentary* report is one that is ____________ ________.

4. List as many words as you can think of that contain the roots *frag, fract,* or *chrono.*

Exercise III Usage Inferences

Choose the answer that best suits the situation.

1. To *divulge* where the treasure was hidden, the angry, captured pirate would have to
   A. know how much it was worth.
   B. have put it there himself.
   C. understand navigation.
   D. be threatened with punishment.

2. Being *duplicitous* is least helpful if a person
   A. wants to have a good recommendation in order to get a better job.
   B. feels it necessary to cheat on an important test in order to pass.
   C. is about to purchase a brand-new car, but doesn't have good credit.
   D. tries to convince a friend to do something the friend doesn't want to do.

3. If your grandmother seems to be *dour*, you might
   A. make the TV louder so she can hear it.
   B. see if you can join in the game she is playing.
   C. ask her to explain what the problem is.
   D. say there is no reason for her to be angry.

Exercise IV Reading Comprehension

Read the selection and answer the questions.

We admire the tragedies of the ancient Greeks; but, to take a correct view of the case, we ought rather to admire the period and the nation in which their production was possible than the individual authors; for though these pieces differ a little from each other, and one of these poets appears somewhat greater and more finished than the other, still, taking all things together, only one decided character runs through the whole.

This is the character of grandeur, fitness, soundness, human perfection, elevated wisdom, sublime thought, clear, concrete vision, and whatever other qualities one might enumerate. Most surprisingly, we find all these qualities not only in the dramatic works that have come down to us, but also in lyrical and epic words, in the philosophers, the orators, and the historians, and in an equally high degree in the works of plastic art that have come down to us. From this we must conclude that such qualities did not merely belong to individuals, but were the current property of the nation and the whole period.

–J.P. Eckermann

1. The speaker states or implies that, as far as the Greeks are concerned, we ought to
   A. admire the poets and playwrights.
   B. admire the people, but reject the poetry.
   C. admire the period and the country, not just individual artists.
   D. reject everything Greek as unfit.
   E. realize that grandeur was fine, but the Greeks lacked intellectual insight.

2. Which of the following is the best statement of the main idea?
   A. Of all the tragedies in Western literature, the tragedies of the Greeks are among the greatest.
   B. That which made Greek literature great was the character of grandeur, fitness, soundness, human perfection, elevated wisdom, sublime thought and clear and concrete vision.
   C. The fact that greatness was evident in not only tragedy but also in poetry, philosophy, history, and the arts indicates that the nation and period is to be more admired than any one individual.
   D. When intellect and culture exist side by side, they will produce a character of grandeur that has a universal appeal.
   E. All of the above are correct.

3. From this selection, it is apparent that the writer
   A. despises the Greeks and their art.
   B. admires some of their work but has a low opinion of other work.
   C. admires the period, their people, and all their art works.
   D. feels that some people have been given too much credit.
   E. does not have any interest in sculpture.

4. The writer states or implies that
   A. the plastic artists are as great as the poets and tragedians.
   B. great literature is elevated wisdom.
   C. great art belongs to everyone.
   D. orators and philosophers frequently are at odds.
   E. human perfection is not possible.

Lesson Nine

1. **emulate** (ĕm′ yə lāt) *verb* to imitate; to try to equal or better
   She advised her son to *emulate* his hard-working, scholarly brother.
   syn: strive

2. **enamored** (ĭ năm′ ərd) *verb* to be in love with
   Alan was so *enamored* of the tall, willowy blond that he stuttered when he tried to speak to her.
   syn: desired, charmed, captivated *ant*: disliked

3. **enhance** (ĕn hăns′) *verb* to increase; to raise to a higher degree or quality
   The soft, shimmering moonlight did much to *enhance* the beauty of the sparkling lake.
   syn: improve, heighten, intensify *ant*: diminish, decrease

4. **enigma** (ĭ nĭg′ mə) *noun* a puzzling or seemingly inexplicable situation, person, etc.
   Because no one knows the thoughts behind that strange grin, Mona Lisa's smile is an *enigma*.
   syn: riddle, secret, mystery

5. **enraptured** (ĕn rap′ chərd) *verb* to be delighted; thrilled
   Elaine was *enraptured* by the performance of the visiting ballet troupe.
   syn: enchanted, charmed, entranced

6. **enunciate** (ĭ nŭn′ sē āt) *verb* to pronounce words clearly and distinctly
   The speech teacher constantly reminded her students to *enunciate* their words carefully.
   syn: articulate, state *ant*: mumble

7. **erudite** (ĕr′ yə dīt) *adj.* scholarly; characterized by wide knowledge
   People should never act more *erudite* than the company they are in; they would appear to be snobs and bores.
   syn: learned, bookish *ant*: unlettered, illiterate

8. **ethnic** (ĕth′ nĭk) *adj.* of or having to do with races or classes of people and their language, culture, history, etc.
   The true American is not from one type of background, but a mixture of countless *ethnic* groups.
   syn: cultural, racial

9. **evince** (ĭ vĭns′) *verb* to show clearly
   In order to *evince* his claim, the scientist performed several tests.
   syn: demonstrate, indicate, prove

10. **evoke** (ĭk vōk′) *verb* to call forth; to draw forth
Pleasant memories of earlier times were *evoked* as we watched the decorated floats parading down Main Street.
syn: summon, elicit, extract

11. **exhort** (ĭg zôrt′) *verb* to use words or arguments to incite one to good deeds
During halftime, the coach *exhorted* his team to play hard and win the game.
syn: urge

12. **exodus** (ĕks′ ə dəs) *noun* a departure, especially in a large group
The defeated tribe made a speedy *exodus* from the war-torn valley.
syn: withdrawal *ant*: entry

13. **expatriate** (ĕks pā′ trē ət) *noun* one who chooses to leave his or her native country
The *expatriate* was greeted by friends and supporters as he stepped off the ship.

14. **expedient** (ĕks pē′ dē ənt) *adj.* the best means to do something under a given set of circumstances, especially if it will bring about personal gain
His action, while not admirable, did prove to be the most *expedient* way to pass the course.
syn: convenient, advantageous *ant*: unfavorable, detrimental

15. **explicit** (ĕks′ plĭs′ ĭt) *adj.* clearly stated
His instructions were *explicit*: do not leave the house for any reason.
syn: exact, precise, definite *ant*: ambiguous, vague

Exercise I Words in Context

Fill in the blanks with the correct vocabulary words needed to complete the sentences.

erudite **explicit** **expedient** **ethnic** **emulate**

A. The new immigrant refused to let his ________________ background hinder him from achieving his goal. He had an ________________ plan as to what he intended to do and how he intended to do it. He wished to ________________ the great inventors who had gone before him and made their fortunes in this new world.

B. She had been to college and was ________________ in matters of philosophy and science; all that remained was for her to think of the most ________________ way to initiate her plan.

exodus **exhorted** **enamored** **enraptured** **enigma**

C. Marcus was totally and completely ________________ by her beauty. He spent whole days thinking of only her. Unfortunately, she was obviously not ________________ of him because she completely ignored him. To his friends, his behavior was something of an ________________. They ________________ Marcus to pull his head out of the clouds and get back to work; they warned him that he would be part of the freshmen ________________ of those who failed the end of the semester if his grades did not improve.

evince **enunciate** **expatriate** **enhance** **evoke**

D. Music, particularly specific songs, may ________________ special memories for a couple; that is why music is often used to ________________ a romantic evening.

E. As an ________________ recently arrived in his new homeland, Kogan wished to ________________ proof of his patriotism. As a result, he, despite his very thick accent, tried to repeat patriotic slogans, but it was both difficult and frustrating to watch him slowly ________________ each and every word.

Exercise II Roots, Prefixes, and Suffixes

Study the entries and answer the questions that follow.

The root *cogn* means "know," "think."
The root *carn* means "flesh."

1. Without using a dictionary, write a definition for each of the following words:

   incognito
   carnivore
   cogitation
   carnivorous
   cognizant
   reincarnate

2. In the phrase "*cogito ergo sum*," *ergo* means "therefore," and *sum* means "I am." What do you suppose the entire phrase means? ________________

3. The word *carnival* refers to a holiday that took place just before the start of Lent. The Latin word *levare* means "to remove." Since Lent was a time when the faithful could not eat meat, what do you suppose *carnival* originally meant?

4. List as many words as you can think of that contain the roots *cogn* or *carn*.

Exercise III Usage Inferences

Choose the answer that best suits the situation.

1. How would a young athlete best *emulate* a star female basketball player?
   A. read about her
   B. practice more
   C. dress similarly
   D. try to meet her

2. If William is an *expatriate*, what can you infer about him?
   A. He does not feel patriotic any more.
   B. He likes commuting to a different state.
   C. He believes in equality for all people.
   D. He enjoys living in a different country.

3. Which would be the best example of an *explicit* comment?
   A. You need to make sure that orchid is never put in direct sunlight.
   B. If you don't follow instructions, something bad will definitely happen.
   C. The boy really disliked the movie about zombies because it was dumb.
   D. One way to write better is by using bigger and more complicated words.

Exercise IV Reading Comprehension

Read the selection and answer the questions.

Conspicuous consumption of valuable goods is a means of reputability to the gentleman of leisure. He, then, not only consumes the staff of life beyond the minimum required to sustain life, but his consumption also undergoes a specialization as regards the quality of the goods consumed. He consumes freely and of the best, in food, drink, narcotics, shelter, services, ornaments, apparel, weapons and accouterments, amusements, amulets and idols, or divinities. As wealth accumulates on his hands, his own unaided effort will not sufficiently display his wealth. Therefore the aid of friends and competitors is brought in by resorting to the giving of valuable presents and expensive feasts and entertainment. Costly entertainment, such as the ball, are peculiarly adapted to serve this end.

–*Thorstein Veblen*

1. What is the best paraphrase of the first sentence?
   A. Buying and eating expensive food helps wealthy gentlemen impress others like themselves.
   B. Purchasing and showing off expensive items allows the wealthy to improve their reputation.
   C. People who have extra leisure time often fill it by purchasing valuable and expensive items.
   D. People who have the ability to show off very valuable possessions will usually try to do so.
   E. Even the poor, who do not possess many valuable goods, are proud of those they do have.

2. The author appears to
   A. envy rich people.
   B. admire rich people.
   C. have no respect for how the rich spend their money.
   D. be very cynical of people.
   E. be angry with people.

3. The author suggests that the main reason people have parties is to
   A. share their good fortune.
   B. show off the excess money they have.
   C. win the favor of their neighbors.
   D. gain political power and influence.
   E. celebrate special events in their lives.

4. The author states or implies that
   A. people buy expensive objects in order to impress others.
   B. competition between people is good for the economy.
   C. wealth should be shared among all people.
   D. the rich are different from the rest of us.
   E. All of the above are correct.

VOCABULARY for the College Bound LEVEL 10

Lesson Ten

1. **expound** (ĕks pound´) *verb* to explain; to set forth point by point; to interpret
   Closing the Bible, the minister *expounded* on the passage he had just read.

2. **expunge** (ĕks pŭnj´) *verb* to erase
   If he can stay out of trouble for one year, his criminal record will be *expunged.*
   syn: blot or strike out

3. **extol** (ĕks tōl´) *verb* to praise highly
   He *extolled* the virtues of his personal hero, Abraham Lincoln.
   syn: eulogize, glorify, laud *ant:* belittle, denigrate, disparage

4. **extradite** (ĕks trə dīt) *verb* to turn a prisoner over to the jurisdiction of another country or state where the crime was allegedly committed
   After two months of incarceration by the Sacramento sheriff, the suspect was *extradited* to Texas.

5. **extraneous** (ĕks trā´ nē əs) *adj.* not belonging; foreign; nonessential
   After producing the chemical compound, the chemical factory poured all *extraneous* material into the river.
   syn: alien, extrinsic, irrelevant *ant:* relevant, intrinsic

6. **extrovert** (ĕks trə vûrt) *noun* a person who is outgoing, friendly, and interested in his or her surroundings, rather than him or herself
   Because he was an *extrovert*, people found him easy to talk to.
   syn: affable *ant:* introvert, withdrawn

7. **exult** (ĕks zŭlt´) *verb* to rejoice over a success or victory
   When the results were announced, the town wildly *exulted* in the team's victory
   syn: triumph

8. **fallacy** (făl´ ə sē) *noun* a false or mistaken idea
   The idea that plants would survive in the dead of winter if someone spoke to them is a *fallacy*.
   syn: error, untruth, falsehood *ant:* truism, fact, axiom

9. **feasible** (fē´ zə bəl) *adj.* reasonable, likely; capable of being carried out
   Given his lack of experience and poor equipment, his plan to compete in the next Olympic games did not seem *feasible*.
   syn: possible *ant:* impossible

10. **fiasco** (fē ăs′ kō) *noun* a complete failure
Because of a breakdown in communications, what should have been a routine naval maneuver ended in a *fiasco.*
syn: debacle, disaster *ant*: success

11. **fickle** (fĭk′ əl) *adj.* likely to change without reason
Because she never liked one band for very long, her friends said she was *fickle.*
syn: vacillating, capricious *ant*: steadfast, determined, loyal

12. **fluctuate** (flŭk′ chōō āt) *verb* to move; to vary irregularly
One could never tell what kind of mood he would be in; he *fluctuated* from extremely friendly to belligerent.
syn: vacillate, waver, sway *ant*: stay, abide, persist

13. **formidable** (fôr′ mĭ də bəl) *adj.* hard to overcome or deal with; causing fear or awe
The pile of thick books and pages of notes on his desk made writing this paper seem a *formidable* task.
syn: menacing, appalling, dreadful *ant*: harmless, feeble, insignificant

14. **frowzy** (frou′ zē) *adj.* dirty, unkempt
The lady's *frowzy* hair looked like Spanish moss because it was so tangled.
syn: untidy, slovenly *ant*: clean, tidy

15. **frugal** (frōō′ gəl) *adj.* not wasteful; thrifty
Because he was a *frugal* man, he always bought day-old bread.
syn: economical

Exercise I Words in Context

Fill in the blanks with the correct vocabulary words needed to complete the sentences.

fluctuated **fickle** **frugal** **fiasco** **expounded**

A. For a long time, the man saved every penny he earned with the plan of buying investments that would make him a millionaire. This ________________ lifestyle cost him his wife and family, but despite this, his ideas never ________________. He felt that his family would be only too happy to return once he had conquered the odds against success. He knew that fortune was ________________ and unkind, so he carefully planned just how his money would grow. However, at the urging of a friend who ________________ at length about a "hot new stock," the man invested all his money in the "hot tip" that went cold. The man sadly watched as his investment plans ended in an abrupt and complete ________________.

extraneous **extolled** **extrovert** **feasible** **fallacy**

B. Though she knew nothing of preserving vegetables, she thought it certainly would be ________________ to freeze the tomatoes. The withered, ruined fruits, however, proved there was a(n) ________________ in her thinking; nevertheless, her enthusiastic classmates ________________ her ingenuity and said that hers was the most interesting science report.

C. Having the personality of a(n) ________________, she found it easy to present her report, even though her experiment had failed. Because she was also a good planner, her report was concise and without any of the ________________ details that made other reports overly long.

formidable **expunged** **frowzy** **extradite** **exult**

D. While he usually did not ________________ in anyone's misfortune, he was happy to see the ________________ woman who had taken his taxi slip on the ice and fall in a puddle.

E. Although he knew there was little chance that the young man's criminal record would be ________________, the jailer did not answer the boy's question directly because of the boy's quick temper and ________________ size. "If," the guard thought, "the state of Arizona wishes to ________________ him and try him for some crimes, he will quickly get a direct answer to his question."

Exercise II Roots, Prefixes, and Suffixes

Study the entries and answer the questions that follow.

The root *agr* means "field."
The suffix *–ous/ose* means "full of."
The root *bell* means "war."
The prefix *ante–* means "before."

1. Without using a dictionary, write a definition for each of the following words:
   antebellum
   belligerent
   bellicose
   anteroom
   agriculture
   agronomy

2. The root *ces/ced* means "to go"; therefore, an *antecedent* is a word which ________________.

3. While an *industrial* society is one characterized by cities and manufacturing, an *agrarian* society is characterized by ________________________.

4. List as many words as you can think of that contain the form *agr* or the prefix *ante–*.

Exercise III Usage Inferences

Choose the answer that best suits the situation.

1. How would a person show that he was an *extrovert*?
   A. by being friendly to others
   B. by reading a book at night
   C. by keeping mainly to himself
   D. by doing very well on the test

2. Which of the following is likely to *fluctuate* most?
   A. a bird in a very small cage
   B. the temperature in winter
   C. the car you drive every day
   D. a movie you've seen four times

3. Why is Martin probably being *frugal*?
   A. He loves eating lots of fast food.
   B. He wants to see his closest friend.
   C. He needs to buy a new computer.
   D. He was recently in a car accident.

Exercise IV Reading Comprehension

Read the selection and answer the questions.

Shakespeare is above all writers, at least above all modern writers, the poet of nature; the poet that holds up to his readers a faithful mirror of manners and of life. His characters are not modified by the customs of particular places that are not practiced by the rest of the world; nor are his characters modified by the peculiarities of studies or professions, which operate but upon small numbers; nor modified by the accidents of transient fashions or temporary opinions: Shakespeare's characters are the genuine progeny of common humanity, such as the world will always supply, and observation will always find. His persons act and speak by the influence of those general passions and principles by which all minds are agitated, and the whole system of life is continued in motion. In the writings of other poets a character is too often an individual; in those of Shakespeare the character is commonly a species.

–*Samuel Johnson*

1. The meaning of the sentence that begins, "Shakespeare's characters…" is that Shakespeare
   A. made his characters speak in a way that his audience could understand.
   B. showed his characters as representing specific types of people.
   C. reflected all of humanity in the depiction of his characters.
   D. portrayed his characters as having more than one side to them.
   E. allowed his characters to express what he himself was feeling.

2. In the last sentence, the author is
   A. criticizing Shakespeare.
   B. complimenting Shakespeare.
   C. neither complimenting nor criticizing Shakespeare.
   D. both criticizing and complimenting Shakespeare at the same time.

3. The author implies or states that
   A. some ancient writer may have been as much a poet of nature as Shakespeare.
   B. most modern poets are not very good.
   C. modern poets lack something.
   D. Shakespeare did not know how to develop characters.
   E. None of the above are correct.

4. "A faithful mirror of manners and of life" is a phrase to indicate that
   A. art is better than life.
   B. life isn't always as good as we hope it to be.
   C. we all see in Shakespeare that which we want to see.
   D. Shakespeare presents people just the way they are.
   E. Both A and B are correct.

Lesson Eleven

1. **frustrate** (frŭs′ trāt) *verb* to disappoint; thwart, baffle
He was so *frustrated* in his unsuccessful attempts to pass the test that he gave up.
syn: balk, hinder *ant*: abet, facilitate, succor

2. **furtive** (fûr′ tĭv) *adj.* done in a stealthy or secretive manner
Not wanting to stare and seem rude, she cast a *furtive* glance toward the odd-looking man.
syn: surreptitious, sneaky *ant*: overt, open

3. **gadfly** (găd′ flī) *noun* a person who annoys others
Do you ask all those questions because you want an answer, or do you just want to be a *gadfly*?

4. **galvanize** (găl′ və nīz) *verb* to startle into sudden activity
A slight motion of the guard's rifle *galvanized* the lazy work crew, and they cleaned the dining hall thoroughly.
syn: stimulate

5. **gamut** (găm′ ət) *noun* the whole range or extent
She ran the *gamut* of emotions as she listened to the speaker's bittersweet story.

6. **gargantuan** (gär găn′ chōō ən) *adj.* of huge or extraordinary size and power
Milltown's players were *gargantuan* compared with the small boys on our team.
syn: gigantic *ant*: tiny

7. **gauche** (gōsh) *adj.* lacking social grace
I felt so *gauche* on the dance floor that I was afraid to ask anyone to dance.
syn: awkward, tactless *ant*: graceful, polite

8. **genial** (jēn′ yəl) *adj.* warm, friendly
Our new neighbors were so *genial* that we felt we had known them for years.
syn: cordial, pleasant, amiable *ant*: unpleasant

9. **grandiloquent** (grăn dĭl′ ə kwent) *adj.* speaking in a pompous style
Although the senator was quite *grandiloquent* during his opening remarks, his audience soon became bored.
syn: pretentious, haughty *ant*: humble, unpretentious

10. **gregarious** (grĭ gâr′ ē əs) *adj.* fond of the company of others; belonging to a flock
Because John was normally a *gregarious* person, his mother became concerned about his exceptionally quiet manner.
syn: sociable, friendly *ant*: unfriendly

11. **grimace** (grĭm′ ĭs) *noun* a facial expression of fear, disapproval, or pain;
verb to make such an expression
The young man *grimaced* when his wife showed him the burned birthday cake.
syn: scowl *ant*: smile

12. **harangue** (hə răng′) *noun* a long, noisy speech or lecture
verb to make such a speech
The father's simple father-to-son talk soon became a *harangue* about the son's failing grades and poor conduct in school.
syn: tirade, declamation

13. **harry** (hăr′ ē) *verb* to torment
Peter was constantly *harried* by feelings of his own inferiority in sports.
syn: harass, pester *ant*: please, delight, enrapture

14. **hearth** (härth) *noun* a fireplace
The rain-soaked travelers huddled near the *hearth* to warm themselves.

15. **heinous** (hā′ nəs) *adj.* hatefully or shockingly evil
The jury was shocked by the *heinous* crimes of which the youth was accused.
syn: abhorrent, horrid *ant*: laudatory, commendable, praiseworthy

Exercise I Words in Context

Fill in the blanks with the correct vocabulary words needed to complete the sentences.

frustrate **furtively** **grimace** **hearth** **grandiloquent** **harangue**

A. After ____________ checking all windows and doors to make certain no one was watching, the man took out the hidden key and unlocked the drawer which held his plans for robbing the bank. As he dressed in his dark clothes, he made a momentary ____________ at the thought that he could possibly be caught; but he quickly dismissed that unhappy thought as improbable. On entering the bank, however, he was surprised to find that the police were there to ____________ his plans. Someone must have told them of his plans.

B. When his wife heard of the stupid thing he had done, she threw the soda she had been drinking against the ____________ and promptly launched into a ____________, which pointed out all of her husband's shortcomings. While it was not a ____________speech, it left no doubt about her opinion of him.

genial **gargantuan** **gauche** **harry** **gregarious** **gamut**

C. The boy had a ____________ appetite. For lunch, he had three large cheeseburgers, two orders of fries, apple pie, and a shake. While he was a ____________ person with a quick smile and a friendly word for everyone, some classmates thought he was ____________ because, besides food, he did, on occasion, put his foot in his mouth.

D. Michael's friends, who ran the ____________ from the delinquent hoodlum to the school genius, were known to ____________ anyone who dared make fun of him. But sometimes they, too, were turned off by his overly ____________ nature and told him to stop showing off or leave the room.

gadfly **heinous** **galvanize**

E. Late in the day when everyone was tired, the director sometimes used tricks to ____________ his crew and get the job finished. Once, he had two actors come on the job site and pretend to get in a furious fight. Then, they committed some ____________ crime that startled the crew. While most of the crew thought it a funny trick, there was always some ____________ who would question the director's tactics and complain loudly about what he did.

Exercise II Roots, Prefixes, and Suffixes

Study the entries and answer the questions that follow.

The root *cosm* means "world," "universe."
The root *cred* means "believe."
The suffix *–ic/id* means "of," "like."

1. Without using a dictionary, write a definition for each of the following words:
   cosmic
   creed
   cosmos
   credentials
   credible
   credence

2. *Micro* means small; therefore, the word *microcosm* refers to a ____________________.

3. Polities refers to a group of citizens; therefore, a *cosmopolitan* person is ____________________.

4. List as many words as you can think of that contain the root *cred.*

Exercise III Usage Inferences

Choose the answer that best suits the situation.

1. What would be a *gargantuan* job?
   A. cleaning a large warehouse
   B. reading a novel in a week
   C. writing a good book report
   D. changing three light bulbs

2. The most likely cause for someone *grimacing* would be
   A. welcoming someone.
   B. straining to lift a weight.
   C. knowing the right answer.
   D. laughing at a television show.

3. Someone would be *furtive* if she
   A. wanted lots of attention.
   B. knew how to play monopoly.
   C. believed in ghosts and zombies.
   D. needed to hide for a while.

Exercise IV Reading Comprehension

Read the selection and answer the questions.

The newspaper is the second hand in the clock of history; and it is not only made of baser metal than those which point to the minute and the hour, but it seldom goes right. Exaggeration of every kind is as essential to journalism as it is to the dramatic art, for the object of journalism is to make events go as far as possible. Thus it is that all journalists are, in the very nature of their calling, alarmists; and this is their way of giving interest to what they write. Herein they are like little dogs; if anything stirs, they immediately set up a shrill bark. Therefore, let us carefully regulate the attention to be paid to this trumpet of danger so that it may not disturb our digestion. Let us recognize that a newspaper is at best but a magnifying glass, and very often merely a shadow on the wall.

–Schopenhauer

1. With which statement would the author of this passage most likely agree?
   A. Newspapers accurately reflect the "clock of history."
   B. Newspapers should strive to be "a shadow on the wall."
   C. "Exaggeration of every kind" is an aim of good reporting.
   D. Journalists emphasize "a shrill bark," rather than reporting facts.
   E. People must "carefully regulate" the reporting in newspapers.

2. The author states or implies that
   A. newspapers cannot be believed.
   B. exaggeration is a necessary part of journalism.
   C. newspapers record history on a daily basis.
   D. Both B and C are correct.
   E. None of the above are correct.

3. The author implies that the problem with newspapers is that
   A. journalists lie in order to sell papers.
   B. journalists chase after stories like dogs.
   C. it is not worth your time to read the newspaper.
   D. newspapers could and should do a better job of reporting the news.
   E. news reports lack perspective because they exaggerate for dramatic effect.

4. The author appears to urge the reader
   A. to forsake the daily newspaper.
   B. to campaign to improve the newspaper.
   C. to read the newspaper but remember its weaknesses.
   D. to seek to regulate the newspaper.
   E. None of the above are correct.

Lesson Twelve

1. **heresy** (hĕr′ ĭ sē) *noun* a belief, usually religious, opposed to the established doctrine
It may sound ridiculous, but in 1633, Galileo was convicted of *heresy* for stating that the earth revolved around the sun.
syn: nonconformity *ant*: conformity, orthodoxy

2. **hoax** (hōks) *noun* something intended to deceive or to fool
The footprints they thought were from Bigfoot turned out to be a *hoax* created by local residents.
syn: deception, fraud

3. **hue** (hyōō) *noun* that quality which makes one color differ from other colors; a particular shade or tint of a given color
We were going to paint the house forest green, but my mother cannot stand that particular *hue*.

4. **humility** (hyōō mĭl′ ĭ tē) *noun* an absence of vanity
There was a lot of *humility* in his voice as he begged the girl to stay.
syn: modesty, humbleness *ant*: haughtiness, arrogance

5. **hurtle** (hûr′ tl) *verb* to dash; to move swiftly and with great force
The big fullback *hurtled* his way through the defensive line and scored the winning touchdown.
syn: plow into

6. **hyperbole** (hī pûr′ bə lē) *noun* extreme exaggeration for effect that is not meant to be taken literally
While his stories are very enjoyable, you cannot believe every word because he does engage in *hyperbole*.

7. **hypercritical** (hī pər krĭt′ ĭ kəl) *adj.* overly critical; too severe in judgment
In his inspection of the barracks, the sergeant was *hypercritical*.

8. **ignominy** (ĭg′ nə mĭn ē) *noun* public shame, disgrace, or dishonor
One simple act of greed made the mayor fall from fame to *ignominy* in a week.
syn: infamy *ant*: renown, eminence, repute

9. **impeccable** (ĭm pĕk′ ə bəl) *adj.* faultless; without flaws
Because her house was always *impeccable*, she won an award.
syn: immaculate, errorless, irreproachable *ant*: incorrect, wrong

10. **implacable** (ĭm plăk′ ə bəl) *adj.* cannot be appeased or pacified
His hatred toward those who had killed his wife and child was *implacable.*
syn: inflexible, relentless, uncompromising *ant*: assuaged

11. **inane** (ĭn ān′) *adj.* without sense or meaning; silly; empty
The *inane* comment about lettuce being an excellent source of protein made the nutritionists in the audience laugh.
syn: foolish, insipid *ant*: significant, meaningful

12. **incarcerate** (ĭn kär′ sə rāt) *verb* to put into prison; confine
He was *incarcerated* for stealing three expensive cars.
syn: imprison *ant*: liberate, emancipate, free

13. **incisive** (ĭn sī′ sĭv) *adj.* sharp; keen; penetrating
Tom's *incisive* answer impressed the teacher so much that she nominated him for the award.
syn: piercing, acute *ant*: superficial, dull

14. **incognito** (ĭn kŏg nē′ tō) *adv., adj.* hiding one's name, rank, or position; disguised
To avoid capture, the escaped prisoner of war threw away his uniform so he could travel *incognito.*
syn: masquerading

15. **indiscreet** (ĭn dĭs krēt′) *adj.* not wise or judicious; imprudent in speech or action
Because of his *indiscreet* behavior at the party, when he revealed company secrets, the boss fired him.
syn: rash, capricious *ant*: circumspect, cautious

Exercise I Words in Context

Fill in the blanks with the correct vocabulary words needed to complete the sentences.

heresy **impeccable** **incarcerated** **incisive** **hue** **indiscreet**

A. The man, although usually a(n) ________________ dresser, wore a gaudy shirt that contained just about every ________________ in the rainbow. His wife said that he had been behaving in an absolutely irrational fashion for several weeks now. His comments about other people, which were once ________________ and helpful she said, now bordered on the ________________, as he frequently made observations of a very personal nature.

B. During the Inquisition in the Middle Ages, many ordinary people were accused of ________________ against the Church. Most were convicted. For this offense, they were lucky if they were only ________________ and not, as often happened, something much worse.

hyperbole **hurtle** **implacable** **incognito** **hoax**
ignominy **humility** **inane** **hypercritical**

C. For years he had felt that the population had heaped ________________ on his good name, and as a result, he developed a(n) ________________ hatred toward everyone in the town. When some boys played a cruel ________________ on him and the woman he loved, he responded by injuring several of them. To say that the townspeople wished to boil him in oil is not to speak in ________________.

D. To say Dave was ________________ is an understatement, for he could find fault with anyone. He even accused our wonderful, humble Pope of lacking ________________.

E. Although the spy wanted to ________________ himself through the crowd and leave the airport as quickly as possible, he knew it would be a(n) ________________ thing to do. Someone who was traveling ________________ could not afford to draw that kind of attention to himself.

Exercise II Roots, Prefixes, and Suffixes

Study the entries and answer the questions that follow.

The root *dorm* means "sleep."
The root *fin* means "end."
The suffix *–ory* means "a place for."
The root *nomen* means "name."
The suffix *–ee* means "one who is."

1. Without using a dictionary, write a definition for each of the following words:
   dormitory
   nomenclature
   dormant
   finale
   nominee
   infinite

2. Something that has an end is limited or ____________________.

3. If one is only *nominally* employed, it means that he or she is employed ____________________.

4. List as many words as you can think of that contain the roots *dorm, fin,* or *nomen.*

Exercise III Usage Inferences

Choose the answer that best suits the situation.

1. Which comment can be thought of as best showing *humility*?
   A. Whatever you are trying to sell me, I am not interested.
   B. I'll do whatever I can to help locate the missing person.
   C. I don't think that I could ever be as good a pianist as you.
   D. Just tell me what you want done to the car, and I'll do it.

2. Which is least likely to be *hurtling* past your vision?
   A. a balloon
   B. a soccer ball
   C. a fast train
   D. an eclipse

3. Why is Maggie *incognito*?
   A. She is fifteen years old today.
   B. She doesn't want to be noticed.
   C. She's proud of her high test score.
   D. She and her mother had a fight.

Exercise IV Reading Comprehension

Read the selection and answer the questions.

A novel will be of a high and noble order the more it represents of inner, and the less it represents of outer, life; and the ratio between the two will supply a means of judging any novel, of whatever kind, from *Tristram Shandy* down to the crudest and most sensational tale of knight or robber. *Tristram Shandy* has, indeed, as good as no action at all; and there is not much in *La Nouvee Heoise* and *Wihem Meister*. Even *Don Quixote* has relatively little, and what there is, very unimportant, and introduced merely for the sake of fun. And these four are the best of all existing novels.

Consider, further, the wonderful romances of Jean Paul, and how much inner life is shown on the narrowest basis of actual event. Even in Walter Scott's novels there is a great preponderance of inner over outer life, and incident is never brought in except for the purpose of giving play to thought and emotion; whereas in bad novels incident is there on its own account. Skill consists in setting the inner life in motion with the smallest possible array of circumstance, for it is this inner life that really excites our interest. The business of the novelist is not to relate great events, but to make small ones interesting.

–Schopenhauer

1. According to the author, what is the difference between "inner life" and "outer life"?
   A. Novels that reflect outer life are the "crudest and most sensational."
   B. Novels that reflect outer life show the "narrowest basis of actual event."
   C. Novels that reflect both lives are the ones that "really excite our interest."
   D. Novels that reflect inner life are those that are just "for the sake of fun."
   E. Novels that reflect inner life are of the "high and noble order."

2. Of Walter Scott's novels, the writer says
   A. there is too little action.
   B. there is too much action.
   C. action is used to give play to inner thought.
   D. they are relatively few and unimportant.
   E. they are the best of the English novels.

3. The author implies that the most important element in a novel is
   A. the theme.
   B. the credibility of the plot.
   C. that the theme not be didactic.
   D. the development of the characters.
   E. historical accuracy.

4. The author states or implies that
   A. *Tristram Shandy* is a good, but crude, novel.
   B. the business of a novelist is business.
   C. good authors do not tell how their characters think and feel.
   D. bad novels have a preponderance of action in them.
   E. Both C and D are correct.

Lesson Thirteen

1. **inert** (ĭn ûrt′) *adj.* having no power to act or move; inactive
The volcano, which had lain *inert* for centuries, suddenly exploded into violent activity.
syn: dormant, passive, idle *ant*: mobile, dynamic

2. **inexorable** (ĭn ĕks′ ər ə bal) *adj.* cannot be moved or influenced by force or argument.
The progress made by the aliens in destroying cities seemed to be *inexorable*, until the hero of the movie showed up.
syn: implacable *ant*: flexible, pliable

3. **inscrutable** (ĭn skrōō′ tə bəl) *adj.* not easily understood; mysterious
I came home to find the most *inscrutable* phone message; I have no idea who called, when, or why.
syn: incomprehensible, enigmatic *ant*: obvious, plain, evident

4. **insipid** (ĭn sĭp′ ĭd) *adj.* without flavor; tasteless; dull; lifeless
Some people find math exciting, but I think that it is simply *insipid.*
syn: flat, vapid, unsavory *ant*: spicy, tempting, zestful, energetic

5. **intrepid** (ĭn trĕp′ ĭd) *adj.* without fear; brave
Because he was an *intrepid* warrior, he received his country's highest award.
syn: dauntless, bold *ant*: cowardly, timid, cautious

6. **irascible** (ĭ răs′ ə bəl) *adj.* easily angered
Because he was so *irascible*, few people liked him, which only contributed to his reputation as a mean-tempered individual.
syn: irritable, ill-tempered *ant*: patient, mild, even-tempered

7. **jaundiced** (jôn′ dĭst) *adj.* prejudiced by envy or resentment; cynical
After the years he spent as a hostage, he had a somewhat *jaundiced* view of Middle Eastern countries.
syn: skeptical *ant*: believing, trusting

8. **jaunty** (jôn′ tē) *adj.* carefree; fashionable, stylish
When my grandfather was young, he considered knickers and knee socks a *jaunty* outfit.
syn: sprightly *ant*: somber, staid

9. **jettison** (jĕt′ ĭ sən) *verb* to throw something away; to get rid of or reject
Heavy suitcases and other personal belongings were quickly *jettisoned* from the damaged boat.
syn: discard

10. **jingoism** (jĭn′ gō izm) *noun* extreme patriotism; favoring an aggressive, warlike foreign policy
The newspapers' and candidates' *jingoism* had led the country into war many times.

11. **jocose** (jō kōs′) *adj.* joking, humorous
He had a *jocose* manner that his bosses did not appreciate.
syn: witty, funny, playful *ant*: serious, morose

12. **juggernaut** (jŭg′ ər nôt) *noun* a terrible destructive or irresistible force
The Nazi *juggernaut* swept through Belgium and into France and met very little resistance.

13. **latent** (lāt′ nt) *adj.* present, but not active; hidden
After he retired, Johnson took up painting and found that he had *latent* artistic talents.
syn: dormant, inert, potential *ant*: manifest, distinct

14. **laudable** (lô′ də bəl) *adj.* worthy of praise; commendable
The citizen's heroic actions in saving the child from the burning building were *laudable*.
syn: honorable, admirable *ant*: abhorrent, base

15. **lethargy** (lĕth′ ər jē) *noun* lack of energy; drowsiness, disinterest
His *lethargy* was understandable at last; the doctor said it was caused by a severe bout of depression.
syn: torpor, apathy, lassitude *ant*: vigor, vitality, liveliness

Exercise I Words in Context

Fill in the blanks with the correct vocabulary words needed to complete the sentences.

irascible **jaunty** **laudable** **latent** **lethargy**

A. Most people in the town admired him. In his sleek sports car with his fashionable, designer clothes, he presented a carefree, ________________ image. Those who knew him well, though, said he had a(n) ________________ temper which could erupt in a tirade of bitter words.

B. Although usually very energetic, sometimes Janet would mope around the house, almost in a state of ________________. On these days, she could be quite ________________ and would snap at anyone who spoke to her. But her many generous gifts to the community and other ________________ acts of kindness were reason enough for most of us who knew her to forgive these lapses.

jingoism **jaundiced** **inscrutable** **jocose** **insipid** **intrepid**

C. Although he had proven himself to be a(n) ________________ warrior, the general's ________________ speeches generally bored his audiences. This night, however, his audience of ultra-right nationalists responded enthusiastically to his ________________ and saber rattling.

D. While her smile was certainly beautiful, there was also an air of mystery about it which gave her a(n) ________________ look. For these reasons some of the other women regarded her with a somewhat ________________ eye. But even in the face of their rude comments, she never lost her ________________ manner and positive attitude.

inert **jettison** **inexorable** **juggernaut**

E. Allan moved through the recently acquired company like a(n) ________________, knocking aside anyone who got in his way. One employee sarcastically said, "So, this must be the ________________ wave of the future against which mere mortals dare not stand. In your effort to breathe new life into this ________________ shipping company, I hope you don't ________________ the good with the bad."

Exercise II Roots, Prefixes, and Suffixes

Study the entries and answer the questions that follow.

The root *fac/fact/fect/fic* means "make," "do."
The root *grat* means "please."
The suffix *–tude* means "the state of."
The root *mot/mov* means "to move."

1. Without using a dictionary, write a definition for each of the following words:

   factory
   congratulations
   gratitude
   motivation
   remote
   demote

2. If you can do something easily, you are said to be ____________________.
   If you make it easy for someone else to do, you ____________________ the action, in which case, you would be called a ____________________.

3. A machine that *makes* a likeness of something is called ____________________.

4. List as many words as you can think of that contain the roots *fac/fact/fect/fic,* or *grat.*

Exercise III Usage Inferences

Choose the answer that best suits the situation.

1. Which of the following best describes a proper description of *inert*?
   A. The ant colony went searching for more food.
   B. My dad falls asleep in the same chair every night.
   C. He's a good player, just not good enough to start.
   D. People enter the museum from any of three doors.

2. Which is the best example of a *juggernaut*?
   A. a moving tank
   B. a moving airplane
   C. a moving van
   D. a moving horse

3. The most *laudable* thing Norman ever did was
   A. graduate from a local college.
   B. help his family get out of debt.
   C. discover the cure for a disease.
   D. win lots of money in the lottery.

Exercise IV Reading Comprehension

Read the selection and answer the questions.

Style is the face of the mind, and a safer index to character than the face. To imitate another man's style is like wearing a mask, which, be it ever so fine, is not long in arousing disgust and abhorrence, because it is lifeless; so that even the ugliest living face is better. Hence those who write in Latin and copy the manner of ancient authors may be said to speak through a mask; the reader, it is true, hears what they say, but he cannot observe their face, so he cannot see their style. With the Latin works of writers who think for themselves, the case is different, and their style is visible. Further, the language in which a man writes is the face of the nation to which he belongs; and here there are many hard and fast differences, beginning from the language of the Greeks down to that of the Caribbean islanders.

–*Schopenhauer*

1. The author dislikes a writer who wears a mask because
   A. real feelings remain hidden.
   B. a mask has no life within.
   C. even an ugly face has beautiful qualities.
   D. writers who used Latin wore them.
   E. it hides the author's true opinion.

2. The author states or implies that
   A. writers from the same country share the same style.
   B. the ancient Latin authors were inferior to modern writers.
   C. writers who copy the style of the ancient Latin authors do not show their own.
   D. All the above are correct.
   E. Both A and C are correct.

3. By "style" the author means
   A. the way a person dresses.
   B. the way an author thinks and uses words.
   C. the way a person carries him or herself.
   D. the appearance on one's face.
   E. Both B and D are correct.

4. The problem with copying another's style is
   A. you mask your own thoughts.
   B. a style that imitates another is easily recognized and arouses disgust.
   C. your own language does not come through.
   D. All of the above are correct.
   E. None of the above are correct.

Lesson Fourteen

1. **levity** (lĕv´ ĭ tē) *noun* lightness or gaiety of disposition; lack of seriousness
An air of *levity* remained long after the comedian left the stage.
syn: frivolity *ant:* sobriety, somberness

2. **lexicon** (lĕks´ ĭ kŏn) *noun* a dictionary; a special vocabulary
Having been a gang member as a youth, Carl was familiar with the *lexicon* of the streets.

3. **libation** (lī bā´ shən) *noun* an alcoholic drink
The guests were offered a small *libation* before dinner was served.

4. **liege** (lēj) *noun* a lord, master, or sovereign
While the servants pledged their loyalty to the *liege*, they did not always like or respect him.

5. **magnanimous** (măg năn´ ə məs) *adj.* noble; generous in forgiving; free from petty feeling or acts
Allowing the man who had insulted him to sit at the same table during dinner was a *magnanimous* gesture on Robert's part.
syn: gallant *ant:* ignoble, vindictive

6. **marital** (măr´ ĭ təl) *adj.* having to do with marriage
The presence of *marital* problems does not mean the marriage needs to end in divorce.
syn: nuptial, matrimonial, conjugal *ant:* single

7. **mercenary** (mûr´ sə nĕr ē) *noun* one who works only for money, especially a hired soldier
Fighting to support a cause or ideal is one thing; but when a *mercenary* kills someone, he is no better than a murderer.

8. **meticulous** (mĭ tĭk´ yə ləs) *adj.* extremely careful about small details
With *meticulous* care, he carved a miniature doll house for his daughter.
syn: fastidious, fussy *ant:* sloppy, careless, remiss

9. **motley** (mŏt´ lē) *adj.* made up of different, dissimilar parts; being of many colors
The International Club was certainly a *motley* bunch of individuals.
syn: disparate, various *ant:* uniform, homogeneous, similar

10. **mundane** (mŭn dān´) *adj.* ordinary, common; earthly, not spiritual
He thought of himself as too much of an artist to deal with *mundane* things such as earning a living.
syn: worldly, secular *ant:* sublime, exceptional

11. **murky** (mûr′ kē) *adj.* gloomy, dark, cloudy
He couldn't think straight; his mind was too *murky* and filled with doubts.
syn: somber, dismal, dingy *ant*: radiant, lustrous, sparkling, clear

12. **myriad** (mĭr′ ē əd) *adj.* related to a very large number; of a highly varied nature
After *myriad* questions had been answered, the witness was excused.
syn: countless, innumerable

13. **naïve** (nä ēv′) *adj.* simple in nature; not affected; innocent simplicity; childlike
Old movies usually portray country girls in the city being *naïve* and vulnerable.
syn: unsophisticated, unsuspecting *ant*: sophisticated, artful, cunning

14. **nocturnal** (nŏk tûr′ nəl) *adj.* having to do with the night; occurring at night
Owls and other creatures that sleep during the day are *nocturnal*.
syn: nightly *ant*: diurnal

15. **novice** (nŏv′ ĭs) *noun* a beginner; one who is new or inexperienced
The older lawyer took the *novice* under his wing and taught her the ropes.
syn: pupil, disciple, apprentice *ant*: master, exemplar

Exercise I Words in Context

Fill in the blanks with the correct vocabulary words needed to complete the sentences.

marital **meticulous** **naïve** **motley**

A. Today's modern science fiction movie must contain certain elements in order to be successful. First of all, to be believable, there must be a ________________ cast of humans and aliens who interact together. The movie usually has a ________________, young hero, who is not interested in personal gain, but in the success of some noble cause. He or she will be joined by an older cynical hero, who is generally opposed by the villain. The hero, after paying ________________ attention to the villain's methods, tries to outmaneuver him. Of course, in the end, the hero succeeds. There is also the love interest, who flies off with the hero; the audience assumes the two will spend the rest of their lives in ________________ bliss.

mundane **novice** **mercenary** **lexicon** **nocturnal** **murky**

B. While we do not think of rabbits as ________________ animals, in our neighborhood you see more rabbits at night or in the ________________ hours of dawn than you see in daylight hours.

C. Some young men read magazines like *Soldier of Fortune* and see themselves as ________________ soldiers fighting wars for people who will pay them large sums of money. These men cannot stand the thought of entering the ________________ world of work on an assembly line or in a factory. Little do they realize that in any army the ________________ soldier is, to use a term from the ________________ of the military, little more than "cannon fodder."

myriad **libation** **liege** **levity** **magnanimous**

D. While the king thought of himself as a well-loved ________________ of his people, he nevertheless employed a poison tester to sample any ________________ before he drank it himself. That was just one of the ________________ ways he had to protect himself.

E. Despite the atmosphere of ________________ at the party, everyone knew that the boss was not the ________________ type of person who would overlook a humorous jab at his person or dignity.

Exercise II Roots, Prefixes, and Suffixes

Study the entries and answer the questions that follow.

The root *hydr* means "water."
The root *junct* means "join."
The prefix *de–* means "down," "away from," "about."
The prefix *dis/di/dif–* means "apart," "not."

1. Without using a dictionary, define the following words:
   dehydration
   disjointed
   juncture
   hydrophobia
   conjunction
   hydroelectric

2. *Hydraulics* is a branch of physics having to do with ______________________________.

3. *Therm* is a root that means "heat"; therefore, *hydrothermal* has to do with ____________________.

4. List as many words as you can think of that contain the roots *hydr* or *junct*.

Exercise III Usage Inferences

Choose the answer that best suits the situation.

1. In which situation is someone depicted as being a *novice*?
   A. Jeremy is the star of the champion debate team.
   B. Doug is helping someone learn how to do algebra.
   C. Rachel is helping with her brother's homework.
   D. Chrissie is finally learning how to print neatly.

2. Which group of words would best describe a *meticulous* person?
   A. happy, generous, and concerned with others
   B. cheap, unfriendly, and loud in most places
   C. careful, neat, and clean almost all the time
   D. worried, nervous, and unsure with strangers

3. What would be the most likely reason that the water was *murky*?
   A. Hundreds of fish were swimming in it.
   B. A severe storm just unsettled the mud.
   C. Everyone watched the shark swim by.
   D. The sun was making it shine brightly.

Exercise IV Reading Comprehension

Read the selection and answer the questions.

Some writers try to make the reader believe that their thoughts have gone much deeper than is really the case. They say what they have to say in long sentences that wind about in a forced and in an unnatural way; they coin new words and write sentences which go round and round the thought and wrap it up in a sort of a disguise. They tremble between the two separate aims of communicating what they want to say and of concealing it. Their object is to dress up an idea so it may look learned, in order to give people the impression that there is very much more in it than for the moment meets the eye. They either jot down their thoughts bit by bit, in short, ambiguous sentences, which apparently mean much more than they say; or else they hold forth with a deluge of words and the most intolerable diffusiveness, as though no end of fuss were necessary to make the reader understand the deep meaning of their sentences, whereas it is some quite simple if not actually trivial idea; examples of these writings may be found in the popular philosophical manuals of hundreds of miserable dunces.

–Schopenhauer

1. Which is one thing the author does not mention about philosophical writings?
   A. Philosophical writings contain very deep thoughts.
   B. Philosophical writings often contain long sentences.
   C. Philosophical writings disclose and hide the author's ideas.
   D. Philosophical writings reflect thoughts of unhappy fools.
   E. Philosophical writings contain many made-up words.

2. The author states or implies that some writers
   A. try to communicate and conceal at the same time.
   B. use long sentences and unfamiliar words to make their thoughts appear deep.
   C. pretend to be deep thinkers, but their thoughts are really shallow.
   D. dress up their writing in order to impress other people.
   E. All of the above are correct.

3. It appears that this writer thinks
   A. all authors are frauds.
   B. many books about popular philosophy are not worth reading.
   C. the study of philosophy is a waste of time.
   D. one might become a better writer by studying philosophy.
   E. Both B and D are correct.

4. The word *ambiguous* must mean
   A. short and concise.
   B. long and diffuse.
   C. having a meaning known only to the author.
   D. not having a meaning at all.
   E. not having a precise meaning.

VOCABULARY *for the* College Bound
LEVEL 10

Lesson Fifteen

1. **noxious** (nŏk′ shəs) *adj.* harmful to the health
There was a *noxious*, overpowering smell in the dimly lit room.
syn: injurious, dangerous *ant*: wholesome

2. **nuance** (nōō′ äns) *noun* a delicate variation in tone, color, meaning, expression
There were *nuances* in the president's later speeches that only the sharpest of listeners picked up on.

3. **obese** (ō bēs′) *adj.* extremely fat
Though people don't usually recognize it, Santa Claus is actually *obese*.
syn: stout, corpulent, rotund *ant*: emaciated, slender, gaunt

4. **obstreperous** (ŏb strĕp′ ər əs) *adj.* boisterous; unruly
The *obstreperous* mob was finally subdued with an icy blast from the fire hose.
syn: noisy, uncontrolled *ant*: calm, obedient

5. **odium** (ō′ dē əm) *noun* hatred; the state of being hated
Even though Roosevelt had to deal with Stalin to win WWII, he regarded the leader with great *odium* because of the man's abuses of Russian citizens.
syn: anathema, abhorrence *ant*: love, adoration

6. **officious** (ə fĭsh′ əs) *adj.* offering unnecessary and unwanted advice or service
The butler's *officious* treatment of the other servants caused many of them to complain.
syn: meddlesome, interfering *ant*: retiring, reticent

7. **ominous** (ŏm′ ə nəs) *adj.* threatening; predicting evil
We went on our picnic despite the *ominous* rain clouds.
syn: foreboding, sinister *ant*: comforting

8. **omniscient** (ŏm nĭsh′ ənt) *adj.* having unlimited knowledge; knowing everything
The narrator who explains to the reader what the characters are thinking or what is happening in more than one place at one time is called an *omniscient* narrator.
syn: all-knowing

9. **ostensible** (ŏ stĕn′ sə bəl) *adj.* apparent, pretended
The *ostensible* reason for his actions—charity—was not his real reason, which was greed.
syn: probable, evident

10. **ostracize** (ŏs′ trə siz) *verb* to banish; to shut out from a group or society by common consent
When Tom married someone of a different religion, the tight little community *ostracized* him.
syn: exile, blacklist *ant*: welcome, accept

11. **pandemonium** (păn də mō´ nē əm) *noun* a wild disorder, noise, or confusion
With the teacher gone, the climate of the room quickly changed from quiet talking to *pandemonium*.
syn: chaos, tumult, din *ant*: tranquility

12. **parsimonious** (pär sə mō´ nē əs) *adj.* too economical; stingy
Ebenezer Scrooge was a *parsimonious* old man who treated everyone with contempt.
syn: frugal, thrifty, cheap *ant*: extravagant, lavish

13. **penitent** (pĕn´ ĭ tənt) *adj.* expressing sorrow for having sinned or done wrong
Because of the boy's *penitent* comments of remorse, the judge was easier on him than she usually was on young people who broke the law.
syn: sorry, ashamed, remorseful *ant*: unashamed

14. **pernicious** (pûr´ nĭsh´ əs) *adj.* causing injury; evil or wicked
While doctors today say that running is beneficial, years ago some people thought that running had a *pernicious* effect on the heart.
syn: detrimental, destructive *ant*: wholesome, beneficial

15. **pertinent** (pûr´ tn ənt) *adj.* having to do with what is being considered; relevant
He didn't mind interruptions as long as what was said was *pertinent* to the topic at hand.
syn: appropriate *ant*: unrelated

Exercise I Words in Context

Fill in the blanks with the correct vocabulary words needed to complete the sentences.

ostracize **obstreperous** **pandemonium** **pertinent**

A. Because of acts of vandalism and other ________________ behavior, the club members felt it necessary to ________________ Carl from their group. They were tired of the ________________ caused by his senseless acts. Collecting all the ________________ information they could find, they went before the club's disciplinary board.

omniscient **obese** **parsimonious** **nuance** **odium** **pernicious** **ominous**

B. Although Uncle Bob now had plenty of money, the ________________ ways of his earlier days still had a strong hold on him; spending a dollar was never a painless task for him. His nephew, hoping to discredit his uncle, started ________________ rumors, not so much by what he said directly, but more so in the ________________ of his comments.

C. The sound of thunder and the black clouds to the north were ________________ signs, but we decided to go camping anyway. Most of us were not too glad about the idea, but our scout leader, who considered himself ________________, said there was no chance of bad weather, so we went. However, when it began to pour rain and he slipped and injured his leg, we had to carry him down the trail. From that moment, we regarded this ________________, 350-pound person with ________________.

ostensible **penitent** **noxious** **officious**

D. Unfortunately, the leading doctor at the hospital was thought of as a(n) ________________ old fool who casually insulted you and then assumed an insincere, ________________ expression if you objected to his comment.

E. While the scientist's clothing suggested that the ________________ reason for his trip to the lake was for fishing, he was really there to investigate a report on ________________ fumes that were being emitted from the mill.

Exercise II Roots, Prefixes, and Suffixes

Study the entries and answer the questions that follow.

The root *loqu/locut* means "speak," "talk."
The root *pend/pens* means "hang."
The root *gest* means "carry," "bring."
The suffix *–cy* means "the state or position of."

1. Without using a dictionary, define the following words:

   elocution
   pendant
   loquacious
   dependency
   eloquent
   gestation

2. Because of the photo finish, the outcome of the horse race was still ________________.

3. A *gesture* is a motion of the body or a part of the body to express or emphasize ideas, emotions, etc. It, too, comes from the root *gest.* How is the word *gesture* related to this root?

4. List as many words as you can think of that contain the roots *loqu, locut,* or *gest.*

Exercise III Usage Inferences

Choose the answer that best suits the situation.

1. What is potentially the most *noxious* part of a chemistry lab?
   A. the equipment
   B. the experiments
   C. the professor
   D. the chemicals

2. Which movie description is most *ominous*?
   A. Watch the families playing together until the food fight breaks out at the BBQ.
   B. Laugh as the three little kids try to impress everyone with their driving skills.
   C. See the amazing true story of how the dinosaurs ruled the land and then vanished.
   D. Be careful because the murderers travel far and wide to claim their next victims.

3. Which person is showing how *parsimonious* he is?
   A. He bought a book, read it, and then returned it for a full refund.
   B. He bought a car, drove it, sold it to a friend, and lost money.
   C. He bought an airplane ticket, flew first class to Hawaii, and stayed.
   D. He bought a smartphone, used it once, and gave it to charity.

Exercise IV Reading Comprehension

Read the selection and answer the questions.

Another characteristic of these writers is that they always avoid a positive assertion wherever they can possibly do so, in order to leave a loophole for escape in case of need. Hence given the choice, they never fail to choose the more abstract way of expressing themselves. Intelligent people, on the other hand, use the more concrete word, because the concrete brings things more within the range of actual demonstration, which is the source of all evidence.

There are many examples that prove this preference for abstract expression; a particularly ridiculous example is afforded by the use of the *verb* "to condition" in the sense of to cause or to produce. People say to condition something instead of to cause it, because being abstract and indefinite it says less; it affirms that A cannot happen without B, instead of that A is caused by B. Thus a back door is always left open; this suits people whose knowledge of their own incapacity inspires them with a terror of all positive assertion; and to make it worse, this tendency is immediately imitated—a fact proven by the rapid way in which it spreads. The Englishman uses his own judgment in what he writes as well as in what he does; but this is less true of the Germans. The consequence of this state of things is that the word "cause" has of late almost disappeared from the language of literature, and people talk only of condition. The fact is worth mentioning because it is so characteristically ridiculous.

–Schopenhauer

1. Which phrase or sentence means essentially the same as, "Thus a back door is always left open"?
   A. a terror of all positive assertion
   B. this preference for abstract expression
   C. People talk only of condition.
   D. Leave a loophole for escape.
   E. Never fail to choose the more abstract way.

2. The author states or implies that the writer who uses abstract language is
   A. destined to be better understood.
   B. destined to be popular with the masses.
   C. not confident of his own opinions.
   D. the more intelligent writer.
   E. usually a poet rather than novelist.

3. Shopenhauer states or implies that
   A. weak writers write in abstractions.
   B. good writers use concrete words.
   C. "these writers" are not writers the author likes.
   D. the writers he speaks of are afraid to commit themselves.
   E. All of the above are correct.

4. The author appears to be a man who
   A. has strong opinions.
   B. has few opinions of his own.
   C. is trying to justify himself by attacking others.
   D. is envious of those writers more popular than himself.
   E. Both A and D are correct.

Lesson Sixteen

1. **pique** (pēk) *verb* 1. to damage pride
2. to excite curiosity or interest

1. The old gentleman was *piqued* because he was not given a seat at the head table.
2. Whenever I travel, my curiosity is *piqued*; then I must study all about where I am going.

2. **plagiarism** (plā′ jə rĭz ĭzm) *noun* taking another's thoughts or words and using them as one's own
Because his own papers earned him only a "D," he committed a desperate act of *plagiarism*.
syn: theft, piracy *ant*: composition, creation, origination

3. **plebeian** (plĭ bē′ ən) *noun* one of the common people
adj. common or vulgar
1. As a freshman in a new school, Frank knew he was nothing but a *plebeian*.
2. The wealthy watched the football game from warm luxury suites, while the rest of us shivered in the *plebeian* seating of the open stadium.
syn: proletarian, undistinguished *ant*: aristocrat, patrician, distinguished

4. **precocious** (prĭ kō′ shəs) *adj.* developed earlier than usual
Although he was not quite a prodigy, he certainly was a *precocious* piano player.
syn: premature, advanced *ant*: backward, obtuse

5. **predatory** (prĕd′ ə tôr ē) *adj.* inclined to rob or prey on others
The buzzard is a scavenger, but the hawk is a *predatory* animal.
syn: pillaging, despoiling *ant*: nurturing

6. **prowess** (prou′ ĭs) *noun* unusual skill or ability; heroism in battle
His physical *prowess* was matched by his superior mental ability.
syn: dexterity, bravery, valor *ant*: timidity, trepidation

7. **pugnacious** (pŭg nā′ shəs) *adj.* eager and ready to fight; quarrelsome
Because he was so *pugnacious*, he had few friends.
syn: combative, belligerent, aggressive, militant *ant*: placid, peaceful

8. **purloin** (pər loin′) *verb* to steal
They had not planned to *purloin* the jewels, but the temptation was too great.

9. **pusillanimous** (pyōō sə lăn′ ə məs) *adj.* cowardly, fearful
In order to gain the trust of the woman he intended to swindle, Matt acted like the *pusillanimous* victim of a robbery, but it wasn't believable.
syn: fainthearted, timid *ant*: brave, bold

10. **quell** (kwĕl) *verb* to put an end to; to allay or quiet
The police were called out to *quell* the riot.
syn: abate, pacify, subdue *ant*: agitate, aggravate, instigate

11. **quixotic** (kwĭks ŏt′ ĭk) *adj.* foolishly impractical or chivalrous
As a young man he had the *quixotic* notion that he could single-handedly end poverty in the country.
syn: capricious, impractical *ant*: realistic, practical

12. **rabble** (răb′ əl) *noun* a disorderly crowd, a mob; the lowest class of people
The guards had to protect the president from the *rabble* in the streets.
syn: riffraff

13. **rabid** (răb′ ĭd) *adj.* intense; furious or raging
The two opposing parties engaged in a *rabid* struggle for control of the country.
syn: violent, extreme *ant*: calm, tame

14. **raconteur** (răk ŏn tôr′) *noun* a person skilled at telling stories or anecdotes
As a *raconteur*, George had no equal, and he was in constant demand to speak at local gatherings.

15. **raillery** (rā′ lə rē) *noun* good-humored ridicule; banter
I much prefer Johnny's *raillery* to the cynical slurs of that other comedian.

Exercise I Words in Context

Fill in the blanks with the correct vocabulary words needed to complete the sentences.

raconteur **pugnacious** **prowess** **rabble** **plebeians**

A. In her old age, Carole found that she was very popular with young children because of her ability to tell stories. She told tales with such ________________ that she was known as the neighborhood ________________.

B. The ________________ gathered in the plaza were good, honest men who sought only their rights guaranteed by law; the Emperor, however, called them ________________ and told the soldiers to "run them off like the frightened little chickens they are." It was quite a surprise, therefore, when the citizens turned ________________ and refused to leave the plaza.

pusillanimous **precocious** **plagiarism** **rabid** **predatory** **raillery**

C. Although he was used to the ________________ that went on in the office, Tom thought the boss went too far when he said that Tom's wife looked like a ________________ dog. He wished that he were not so ________________, but Tom knew he did not have the courage to confront his boss.

D. As a child, Theresa had always been ________________, and as a result, she graduated from high school at the age of fourteen. At twenty, when Theresa was in graduate school, she submitted a number of stories for publication. When one of the rejected stories appeared in a magazine though, Theresa knew that some ________________ editor had committed ________________ and had stolen the story she had written.

piqued **quixotic** **purloin** **quell**

E. He was a ________________ young man who fought the windmills of bureaucracy and never even noticed that they were not in the least ________________ by his attacks.

F. The thief knew that if he could ________________ the anxieties of the townspeople to the point that they trusted him, he then could ________________ any treasure he wished.

Exercise II Roots, Prefixes, and Suffixes

Study the entries and answer the questions that follow.

The root *man* means "hand."
The suffix *–scent/escent* means "becoming."
The root *nat/nas* means "born."

1. Without using the dictionary, define the following words:

   manacles
   nativity
   ienascence
   innate
   nascent
   manicure

2. Literally, *manual* labor is labor __________________. The word *manufacture* contains the two roots __________________ and __________________ and literally means __________________. The word *manipulation* refers to __________________, and the word *manuscript* literally means __________________.

3. A *mandate* is an order or command. Explain the probable derivation of this word.

4. A *maniac* is a madman, a lunatic. The word comes from the Latin and the Greek word *mania*—"madness," "to rage." So, someone who is *maniacal* is __________________. When we call someone a *monomaniac*, we are saying that his or her madness is focused on __________________.

5. List all the words you can think of that have the suffix *–scent* or *–escent*.

Exercise III Usage Inferences

Choose the answer that best suits the situation.

1. If someone were *pugnacious*, which would he or she most likely not do?
   A. remain quiet when he was being insulted about his hair
   B. continue an argument that she thought she was winning
   C. compete for a starting spot on the school volleyball team
   D. become angry if he felt that the answer he received was a lie

2. What would a teacher most want to *quell*?
   A. a long discussion on Shakespeare
   B. a loud dispute among students
   C. a test that no one was prepared for
   D. a student who asked for a hall pass

3. A *rabid* reader will most likely
   A. dislike reading anything but plays.
   B. stop reading after leaving high school.
   C. read for only ten minutes at a time.
   D. continue to read after being told to stop.

Exercise IV Reading Comprehension

Read the selection and answer the questions.

The first rule for a good style is that the author should have something to say; in fact, this is almost all that is necessary. Ah, how much it means. The neglect of this rule is a fundamental trait in the philosophical writing, and, in fact, in all the literature of my country, especially since Fichte. These writers want to appear as though they had something to say; whereas they have nothing to say. Writing of this kind was brought in by the pseudo philosophers at the Universities, and now it is current everywhere, even among the literary notables of the age. This kind of writing is the mother of that strained and vague style, where there seems to be two or even more meanings in the sentence; it is also the mother of that cumbrous manner of expression, called *le style empese*; it consists in pouring words out like a flood; finally, it is the mother of that trick of concealing the worst poverty of thought under a barrage of never ending chatter, which clacks away like a windmill and quite stupefies one—stuff which a man may read for hours without ever getting hold of a single clearly expressed and definite idea. However, people are easygoing, and have formed the habit of reading page upon page of all sorts of such *verb*iage without having any idea of what the author really means. The writer believes it is as it should be, and fails to discover that he is writing simply for writing's sake.

–*Schopenhauer*

1. What is the most likely meaning for the word *cumbrous*, as it is used in the passage?
   A. not easily handled
   B. easy to understand
   C. without any facts
   D. filled only with ideas
   E. purely philosophical

2. The author states or implies that
   A. Fichte is the cause of much bad writing.
   B. bad writing is generally at vogue in the universities.
   C. most philosophical writing is bad.
   D. philosophical writers cover their lack of thought with poor writing.
   E. All of the above are correct.

3. The author also states or implies that
   A. most readers are ignorant and lazy.
   B. most readers don't understand what they read.
   C. most writers do not realize they have nothing to say.
   D. Both B and C are correct.
   E. A, B, and C are correct.

4. The author says the most important requirement for good style is
   A. a sense of modern rhetoric.
   B. a firm grasp of grammar.
   C. a large and solid vocabulary.
   D. having something to say.
   E. All of the above are correct.

Lesson Seventeen

1. **rancor** (răng´ kər) *noun* extreme hatred or ill will
Although Lou usually did not feel *rancor* toward an opposing lawyer, Whelan's double-dealing had him seething.
syn: animosity, antagonism, resentment *ant:* amity, sympathy

2. **remorse** (rĭ môrs´) *noun* deep regret for a sin or wrongdoing
Ben would have received a heavier sentence, but because of the *remorse* he had expressed, the judge let him off easier than had been expected.
syn: contrition, penitence *ant:* unrepentant

3. **renegade** (rĕn ĭ gād´) *noun* one who deserts a cause and goes over to the other side; a traitor
The Democrats called him a *renegade,* but the members of the Republican Party called him a patriot.
syn: turncoat, defector *ant:* loyalist

4. **retribution** (rĕt rə byōō´ shən) *noun* a just or deserved punishment
As *retribution* for the vandalism, the boys had to spend the weekend picking up litter on the road.
syn: retaliation *ant:* clemency

5. **sanction** (săngk´ shən) *verb* to give approval to
The teacher could not *sanction* the student's habit of copying other people's papers.
syn: authorize, endorse, support *ant:* object, censure

6. **scourge** (skûrj) *noun* a person or thing that causes great trouble or misfortune
Severe diseases that result in many deaths have always been a *scourge* to mankind.
syn: afflict, torment, tribulation

7. **strident** (strīd´ nt) *adj.* harsh or harsh sounding
The woman's *strident* voice began to get on our nerves.
syn: loud, shrill *ant:* quiet, peaceful

8. **taciturn** (tăs´ ĭ tûrn) *adj.* not fond of talking; usually silent
We were amazed when the *taciturn* young man signed up for public speaking.
syn: reticent, reserved *ant:* garrulous, loquacious, talkative

9. **temerity** (tə mĕr´ ĭ tē) *noun* reckless boldness
We couldn't believe he had the *temerity* to speak back to the teacher.
syn: audacity, indiscretion *ant:* caution, circumspection, discretion

10. **terse** (tûrs) *adj.* brief, to the point
The sheriff's *terse* command quickly brought the prisoner to his feet.
syn: concise, succinct

11. **uncanny** (ŭn kăn′ ē) *adj.* weird, strange; mysterious; acute
The boy had an *uncanny* memory for minute details.
syn: unearthly

12. **unctuous** (ŭngk′ cho͞o əs) *adj.* excessively polite
The *unctuous* tone of the salesman's voice made the customers a little uneasy.

13. **verbose** (vər bōs′) *adj.* using more words than are needed; wordy
As soon as I was cornered by my *verbose* cousin, I knew I would be late for my meeting.
syn: garrulous *ant*: terse, concise, succinct

14. **vindicate** (vĭn′ dĭ kāt) *verb* to clear of guilt or blame
Even though he had been *vindicated* of the murder charge, the local people still looked at him suspiciously.
syn: absolve *ant*: convict, blame

15. **vindictive** (vĭn dĭk′ tĭv) *adj.* seeking revenge; bearing a grudge
There was no appeasing his *vindictive* nature once he felt that he had been wronged.
syn: vengeful, spiteful *ant*: forgiving

Exercise I Words in Context

Fill in the blanks with the correct vocabulary words needed to complete the sentences.

temerity **taciturn** **vindictive** **rancor** **remorse**

A. When they asked him to make his speech, he blushed. He was by nature a ________________ man who viewed speech-making as something to be avoided, yet everyone said that his brave comments in taking on the rich factory owners showed great ________________.

B. Barb's boss was a ________________ man who sought to avenge both real and imagined insults. He was greatly feared because his ________________ knew no bounds, and he never expressed any ________________ for the terrible things he said and did.

terse **renegade** **scourge** **strident** **retribution** **vindicate**

C. In that part of the country, it was not the Native Americans, but the ________________ white settlers who were considered a ________________. When these outlaws were caught, ________________ was swift and harsh.

D. The candidate issued a low key, ________________ statement in which he tried to ________________ himself in the eyes of the voter; however, this statement only increased the ________________ comments of his opponents.

sanction **unctuous** **uncanny** **verbose**

E. The headmaster was a(n) ________________ man who was much too polite and willing to give in to parents' demands; once they left, however, he showed that he had ________________ways of taking his frustrations out on the students.

F. While she did not ________________ rude behavior, the principal could not help smiling at the imitation the children did of the ________________ teacher they called "Big Windbag."

Exercise II Roots, Prefixes, and Suffixes

Study the entries and answer the questions that follow.

The root *phil* means "love," "loving."
The root *ocul* means "eye."
The root *mar* means "sea."

1. Without using a dictionary, define the following words:

   philanthropy
   ocular
   philharmonic
   oculist
   maritime
   submarine

2. The root *sophos* means "wise," so a *philosopher* is one who ____________________. On the other hand, the root *moros* means "foolish or fool"; therefore, the literal meaning of *sophomore* is a ____________________.

3. *Phile* is sometimes found at the end of a word. What do you suppose the following people love? *Anglophile, Francophile, bibliophile.*

4. List all the words you can think of that contain the roots *phil*, *ocul*, or *mar*.

Exercise III Usage Inferences

Choose the answer that best suits the situation.

1. If Peggy is *taciturn*, she
   A. believes that what she reads online is true.
   B. does not talk until the teacher calls on her.
   C. complains when her mom serves broccoli.
   D. dislikes it when she has to read a new book.

2. Which comment given in school is most *terse*?
   A. I am probably the only one who got it right!
   B. I can't believe you didn't read the chapter!
   C. Forget it; you don't know either!
   D. I passed!

3. For what would Katrina likely show the greatest *remorse*?
   A. She misplaced her car key.
   B. She came in second in a race.
   C. She bought a dress for the prom.
   D. She insulted her best friend again.

Exercise IV Reading Comprehension

Read the selection and answer the questions.

Studies serve for delight, for ornament, and for ability. The chief use of studies for delight is in privateness and retiring; their chief use for ornament is in discourse; and for ability, they are used in the judgment and disposition of business. For expert men can execute and perhaps judge of particulars, one by one; but for general counsels and the ability to marshal affairs, this comes best from those that are learned. To spend too much time in studies is sloth; to use them too much for ornament is affectation; to make judgment wholly by their rules is the humor of a scholar. Studies perfect nature and are perfected by experience: for our natural abilities are like natural plants that need pruning by study; and studies themselves do give forth directions but they need to be bounded in by experience. Crafty men condemn studies, simple men admire them, and wise men use them; for studies teach not only their own use, but also that there is a wisdom outside them, and above them; this wisdom may be won by observation. Read not to contradict and confute; nor to believe and take for granted; nor to find talk and discourse; but to weigh and consider.

–Francis Bacon

1. According to the author, why should people read?
   A. to gain additional knowledge
   B. to improve a person's vocabulary
   C. to argue about what the author says
   D. to think about the ideas expressed
   E. to believe what the writer states

2. The author's argument implies that
   A. some people read for the wrong reasons.
   B. one can never spend too much time in studies.
   C. by and large studies have no practical use, but they are pleasant to have.
   D. one can make sound judgments based solely on one's studies.
   E. None of the above are correct.

3. The author states that studies
   A. have nothing to do with experience.
   B. are a distraction from work.
   C. may be overused, in which case they are like ornaments.
   D. do reward the bright and encourage the slow.
   E. may be used as the sole basis for all our decisions.

4. Bacon says that it is the humor of the scholar
   A. to argue with everyone.
   B. to study only in order to be able to refute.
   C. to make judgments based only on studies.
   D. to be advised by studies.
   E. Both A and B are correct.

VOCABULARY
for the College Bound
LEVEL 10

Lesson Eighteen

1. **antibacterial** (ăn tī băk tēr′ ēəl) *adj.* having germ-killing properties
noun a substance that kills bacteria
Antibacterial chemicals did not need to be added to the formula of bleach because bleach itself kills most bacteria.

2. **astronomical unit** (ăs trō nŏm′ ĭ kl ū′ nĭt) *noun* a measurement used in astronomy equal to the distance between the earth and the sun; approximately 93,000,000 miles
The distance between the sun and Jupiter, expressed in *astronomical units,* is nearly five, meaning it's almost five times farther away than the earth is.

3. **biodiversity** (bī ō dī vər′ sĭ tē) *noun* the degree of variation of life within a specific environment or species
There is a greater *biodiversity* of fish and corals in the oceans around Indonesia than in any other area of the planet.

4. **botany** (bŏt′ ə nē) *noun* the study of plants
Charles Darwin made his historic voyage to the Galapagos to study the islands' biology and *botany*, report on his findings, and bring back interesting specimens.

5. **cytology** (sī tŏl′ ə jē) *noun* the study of cells
During the course on *cytology*, we learned facts about the various methods of cellular division.

6. **ecosystem** (ē′ kō səs təm) *noun* the grouping of living organisms inhabiting the same environment
Take one element out of an *ecosystem*, and the rest must adapt to the loss; put that organism into a new one, and it may become a dominant force because it has no natural predators.

7. **genetics** (jə nə′ tĭks) *noun* the study of heredity, genes, and inherited traits
Some plants can easily adapt to changes in the environment through a combination of *genetics* and a rapid reproduction rate, while others cannot.

8. **geriatrics** (jər ē ä′ trĭks) *noun* the health care of the elderly
The doctor's ailing grandmother gave him a personal reason to specialize in *geriatrics*.

9. **infectious** (ĭn fək′ shəs) *adj.* capable of being transmitted through disease-causing organisms
Some of the most *infectious* diseases in cattle, like bluetongue, blackleg, and brucellosis, kill thousands of cows each year and cost farmers millions of dollars.

10. **metastasize** (mə tăs′ tə sīz) *verb* to change the form of a cancerous tumor, as in accelerating its growth
When the doctors examined the tumor, they found it had *metastasized* and was too close to the patient's spine to be operated upon.

11. **nucleus** (nōō′ klē əs) *noun* the central and essential core of a cell; a central point or group around which action occurs
In the movie, the scientists bombarded the *nucleus* of a cell taken from a crocodile with laser beams in order to produce enough changes to recreate a dinosaur.

12. **pathology** (păth ŏl′ ə jē) *noun* the study of disease
An examination of the *pathology* of the extremely dangerous Ebola virus reveals that the disease is spread through direct person-to-person contact only.

13. **periodic table** (pēr ē ŏd′ ĭk tā′ bl) *noun* an organized visual display of chemical elements and their properties
The *periodic table* is not arranged alphabetically, but by the number of protons in each element's nucleus.

14. **photosynthesis** (fō tō sĭn′ thə səs) *noun* the process of converting light into energy
It used to be thought that plants are the only organisms that use *photosynthesis,* but some bacteria can do so, too.

15. **solstice** (sōl′ stĭs) *noun* the twice-a-year occurrence—summer and winter— during which the sun is at its greatest distance from the earth
In the Northern Hemisphere, during the winter *solstice*, there are fewer minutes of daylight than on any other day of the year, while the night is the longest.

Exercise I Words in Context

Fill in the blanks with the correct vocabulary words needed to complete the sentences.

periodic table **genetics** **botany** **astronomical units**

A. When the class entered the science lab, the students saw in the front a(n) ____________________ of the elements, a poster showing equations related to physics and calculus, and a scaled down replica of the solar system, with the differences in ____________________ among the planets labeled. They became confused, since they had all signed up for a class in animal ____________________. The teacher walked in and said, "Welcome to 10th grade science. As you can see, from what is in front of you, all science is interconnected. We will even be touching on the history of plant DNA and how it influences ____________________."

nucleus **pathology** **cytology** **geriatrics** **infectious**

B. Because of changes in the immune system as people age, practicing ____________________ requires doctors to learn how to identify an entirely new group of distinct ____________________ diseases that are usually harmless to younger individuals. In addition, doctors will need to become knowledgeable about ____________________ by using a microscope efficiently. Weakening of the cell's ____________________, as well as the cell wall, is a common cause of illness in these patients. Besides these two, however, knowledge of ____________________ and a few courses in how diseases are spread are necessary, if someone is to be successful in this specialized field.

biodiversity photosynthesis ecosystem solstice metastasized antibacterial

C. To make the winter ________________ last for six months, the scientists decreased the hours that the lights were on inside the enormous sealed building. The plants' ________________slowed down. Within a short time, the bugs that depended on the plants for nectar began to die; since they were a major source of food for birds, the reduction in insect numbers caused a huge change in the entire ________________. By the end of a year of experimentation, only three types of insects, two different flowers, and one species of bird remained. The scientists were sure that ________________ would be lost quickly. They theorized that cells had ________________ much faster because of the environmental changes. The experiment ended, the enclosure was sprayed with ________________ gases, and the building was closed forever.

Exercise II Roots, Prefixes, and Suffixes

Study the entries and answer the questions that follow.

The root *path* means "suffering," "emotion."
The prefix *meta–* means "changed, altered."
The root *sol* means "sun."
The suffix *–ious* means "full of," "having to do with."
The root *phot* means "light."

1. Give the literal meaning for the following:

   metamorphosis
   metabolism
   metaphor

2. The prefix *tele–* means "far" or "distant," so a ________________ lens is essential for taking pictures of objects at a distance. ________________ reflections can cause "lens flare" in a photograph, which can be a problem when taking pictures on a sunny day.

3. Chicken pox is a *contagious* disease that can be spread by ________________.

4. List as many words as you can that contain the root *path*.

Exercise III Usage Inferences

Choose the answer that best suits the situation.

1. Which word or phrase would you most likely *not* hear in a discussion of *cytology*?
   A. cell nucleus
   B. the speed of light
   C. causes of mutations
   D. a microscopic examination

2. Which word is most closely related to *pathology*?
   A. illness
   B. stars
   C. weather
   D. plants

3. What is the best example of something that is an *ecosystem*?
   A. an ancient Egyptian tomb being opened for the first time, revealing a previously unknown pharaoh
   B. a restaurant that grows its own vegetables and also composts its own garbage
   C. a college professor uses her own book to teach the class, then uses student essays for her next book
   D. a manufacturer who places a warning on a violent video game, but will sell it to buyers of any age

Exercise IV Reading Comprehension

Read the selection and answer the questions.

Mythology is the science which treats of the early traditions, or myths, relating to the religion of the ancients, and includes, besides a full account of the origin of their gods, their theory concerning the beginning of all things. Among all the nations scattered over the face of the earth, the Hebrews alone were instructed by God, who gave them not only a full account of the creation of the world and of all living creatures, but also a code of laws to regulate their conduct. All the questions they fain would ask were fully answered, and no room remained for conjecture.

It was not so, however, with the other nations. The Greeks and Romans, for instance, lacking the definite knowledge which we obtain from the Scriptures, and still anxious to know everything, were forced to construct, in part, their own theory. As they looked about them for some clue to serve as guide, they could not help but observe and admire the wonders of nature. The succession of day and night, summer and winter, rain and sunshine; the fact that the tallest trees sprang from tiny seeds, the greatest rivers from diminutive streams, and the most beautiful flowers and delicious fruits from small green buds,—all seemed to tell them of a superior Being, who had fashioned them to serve a definite purpose.

They soon came to the conclusion that a hand mighty enough to call all these wonders into life, could also have created the beautiful Earth whereon they dwelt. These thoughts gave rise to others; suppositions became certainties.... The Earth did not exist. Land, sea, and air were mixed up together; so that the earth was not solid, the sea was not fluid, nor the air transparent. Over this shapeless mass reigned a careless deity called Chaos, whose personal appearance could not be described, as there was no light by which he could be seen. He shared his throne with his wife, the dark goddess of Night, named Nyx or Nox, whose black robes, and still blacker countenance, did not tend to enliven the surrounding gloom.

These two divinities wearied of their power in the course of time, and called their son Erebus (Darkness) to their assistance. His first act was to dethrone and supplant Chaos; and then, thinking he would be happier with a helpmeet, he married his own mother, Nyx.

–H. A. Guerber

1. How were the Greeks and Romans different from the Hebrews, according to the author?
   A. The Greeks and Romans worshipped gods, but could not explain "two divinities."
   B. God explained the "creation of the world" to the Hebrews.
   C. The Greeks and Romans could read only portions of "the Scriptures."
   D. The Greeks and Romans believed in "Chaos," a time before the world began.
   E. The Hebrews were "scattered over the face of the earth."

2. Which statement is false?
   A. Nyx was also known as Nox.
   B. Chaos could not be seen.
   C. Nyx was married to Erebus.
   D. Chaos took Erebus' throne.
   E. Nyx was married to Chaos.

3. Which element did not lead the ancient cultures to believe in a superior being?
   A. People had a purpose.
   B. Trees grew from seeds.
   C. Storms raged at sea.
   D. Day became night.
   E. Streams turned into rivers.

4. With which statement would the author most likely agree?
   A. Complete knowledge of the world was impossible for the ancient people.
   B. The marriage of a child to its mother is morally wrong, even if they both are gods.
   C. The worship of one God is justified, but the worship of many gods is not.
   D. The Greeks believed that sea, air, and land were never together.
   E. Mythology rarely has an explanation of the creation of the earth.